1

Phonics PARTY

Single Letter Sounds

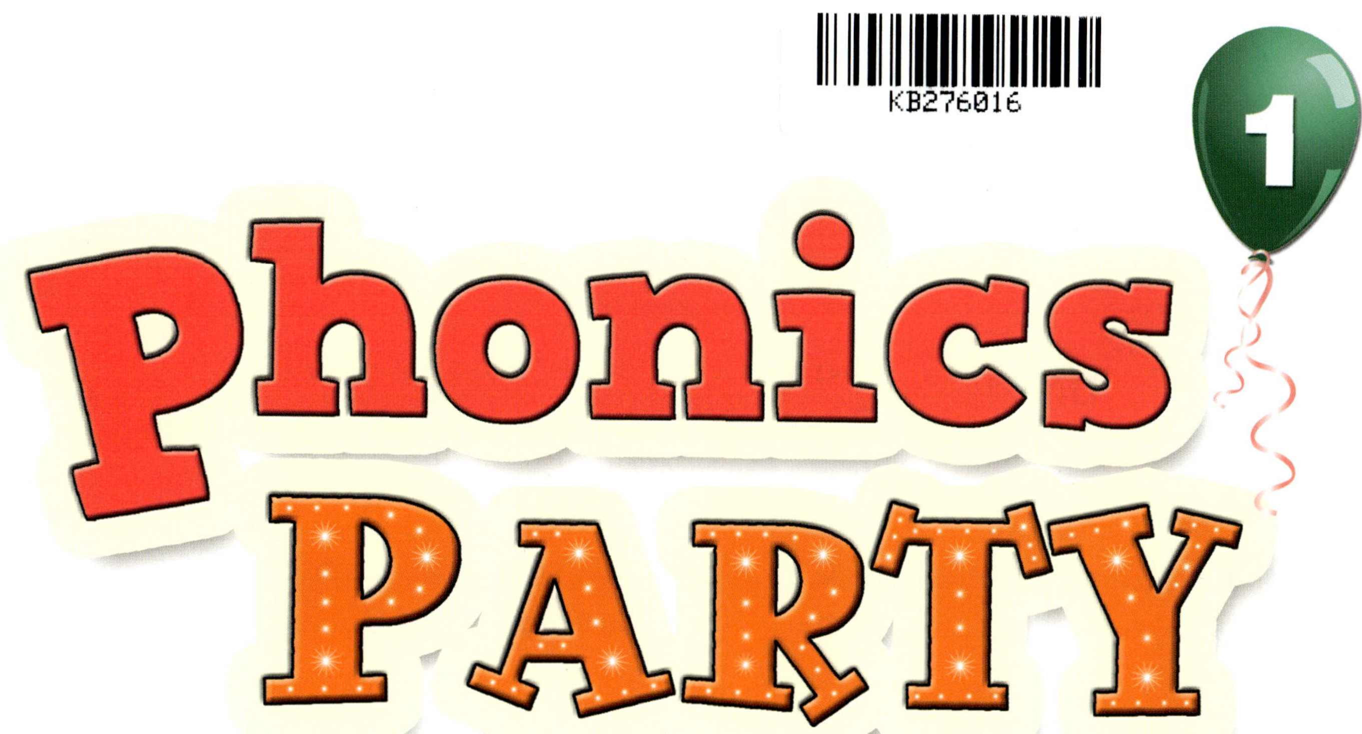

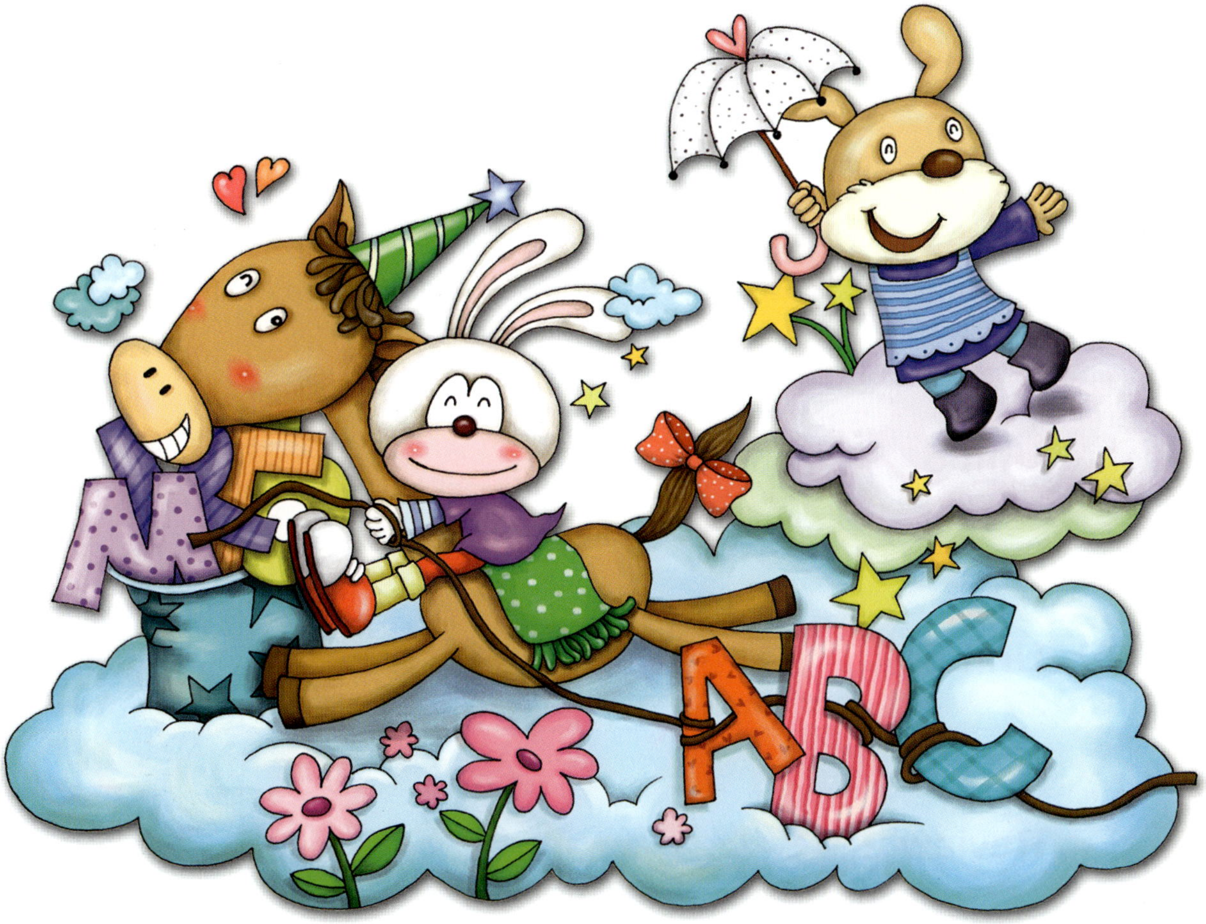

WorldCom Edu

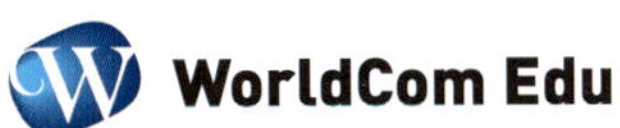

CONTENTS

Book 1

Phonics PARTY 1

A a B b

Let's sing **A a** and **B b**. MP3 **01** / Unit 1

A and B

Date . . .

2. Listen

Listen and repeat **A a** and **B b.** MP3 **02** / Unit 1

A 

A 

a 

a 

B 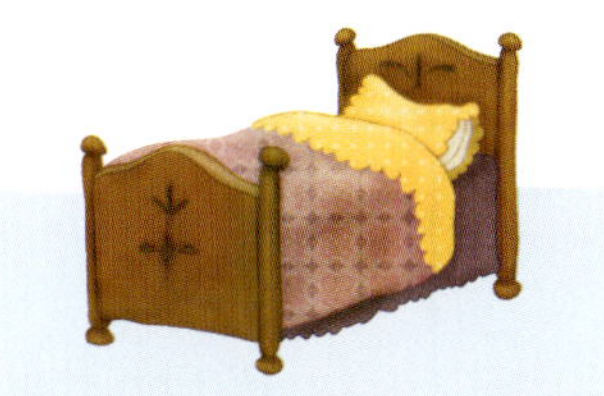

B 

b 

b 

Trace and write **A** and **a**.

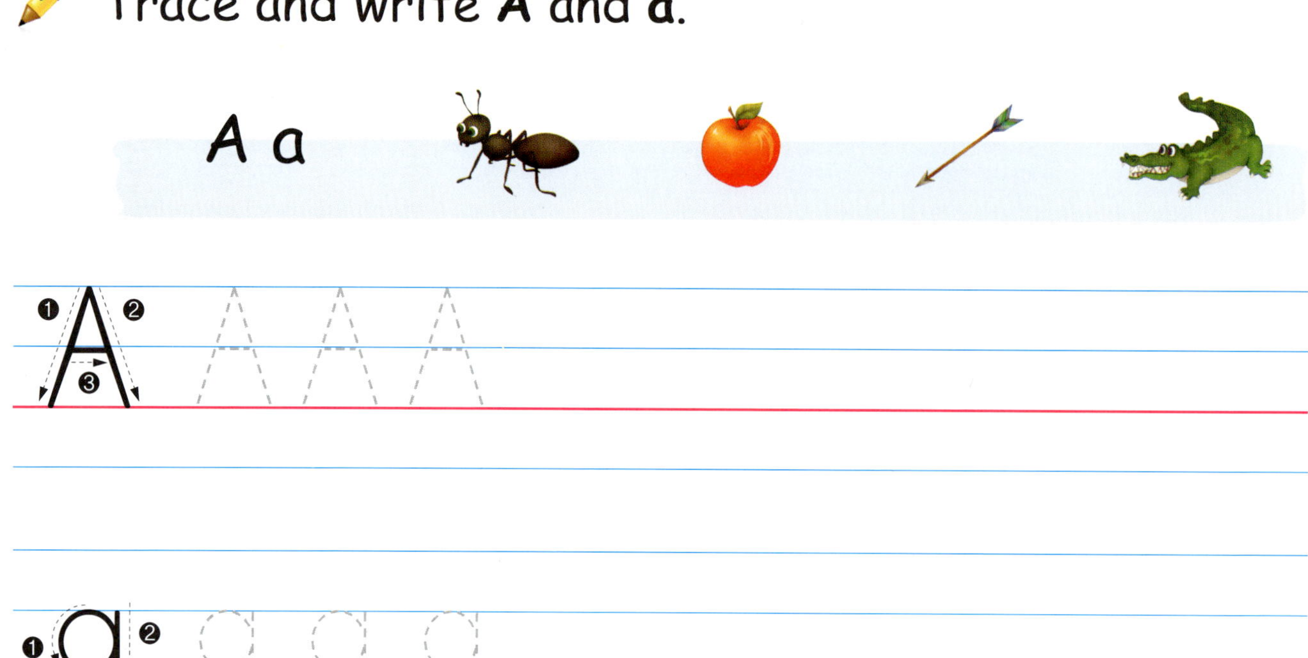

Listen and write the beginning letter. MP3 **03** / Unit 1

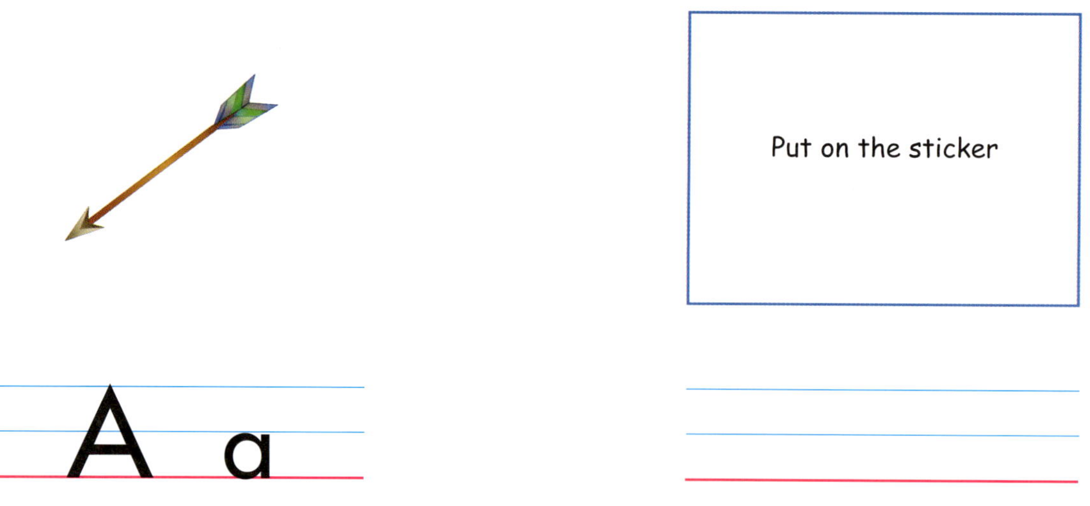

Date . . .

Trace and write B and b.

Listen and write the beginning letter. 04 / Unit 1

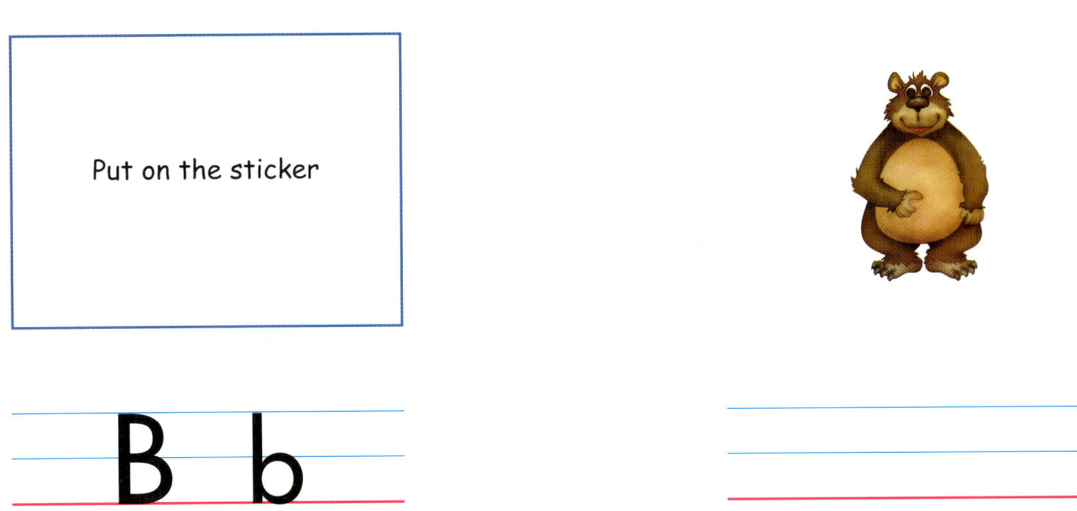

4. Speak

Say the beginning letters.
Put on the stickers.

1 

2    

5. Remember

Circle the letters.

A	H	A	K	T	A	A	L
a	a	c	a	a	e	o	a
B	P	B	B	D	B	E	B
b	b	d	b	f	b	p	b

Date . . .

a is for

a is for

A a is for  

Aa a

b is for 

b is for 

B b is for 

Bb b

C c D d

Let's sing **C c** and **D d.** MP3 **06** / Unit 2

C and D

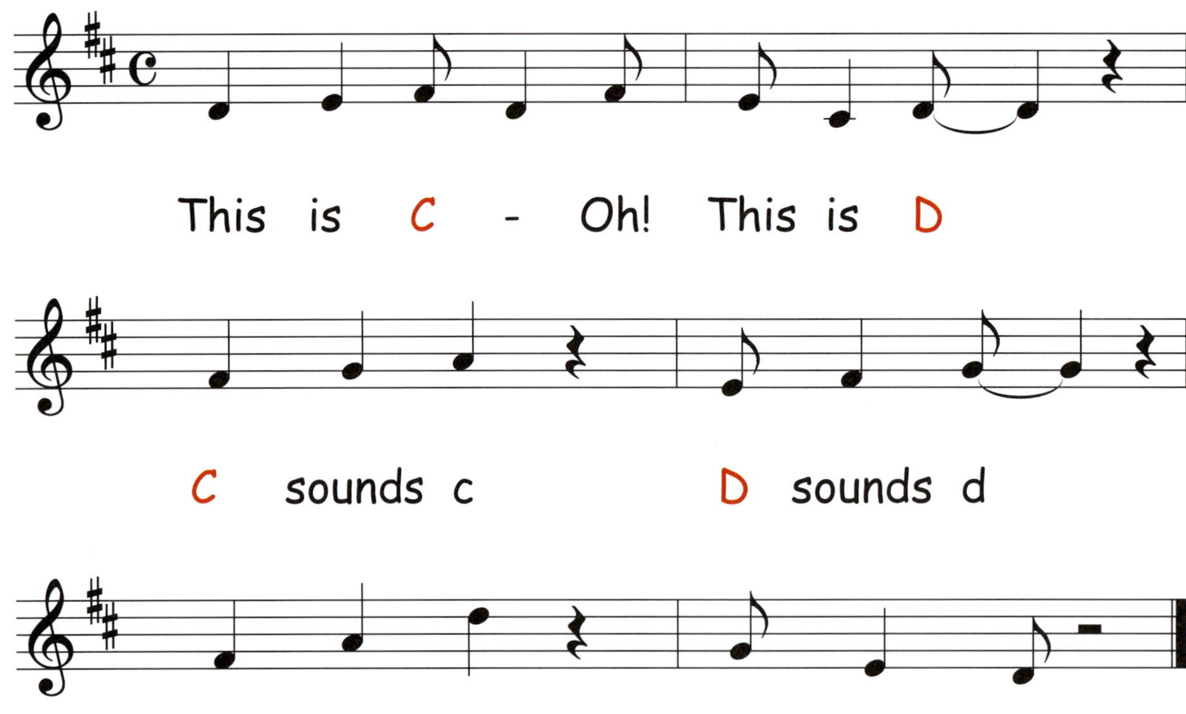

Date . . .

2. Listen

 Listen and repeat C c and D d. MP3 07 / Unit 2

C  C 

c  c 

D  D 

d  d 

3. Write

 Trace and write **C** and **c**.

C c

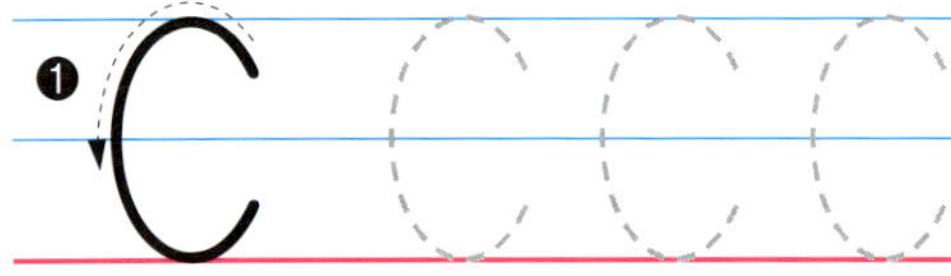

 Listen and write the beginning letter. **08** / Unit 2

Put on the sticker

C c

Date . . .

Trace and write **D** and **d**.

Listen and write the beginning letter.

MP3 09 / Unit 2

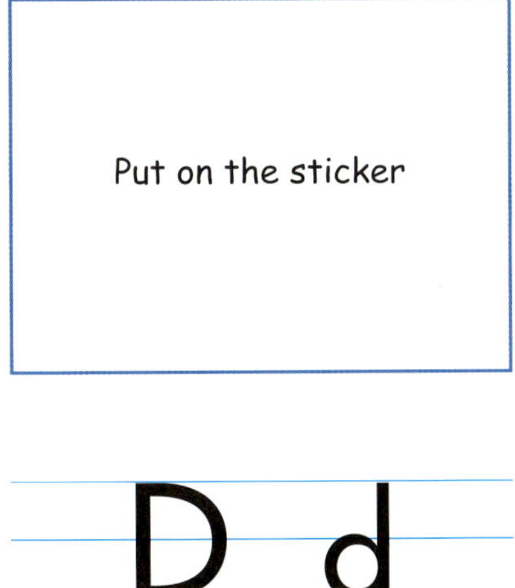

4. Speak

Say the beginning letters.
Put on the stickers.

1

2

5. Remember

Circle the letters.

C	C	D	O	C	C	G	C
c	s	e	c	u	c	o	c
D	D	D	B	D	P	D	E
d	b	j	d	r	d	d	p

Date . . .

6. Chant

Let's chant C c and D d. MP3 10 / Unit 2

c is for 

c is for 

C is for  

Cc c

d is for 

d is for 

D is for  

Dd d

E e F f

PP1-03
MP3

Let's sing E e and F f. .MP3 11 / Unit 3

E and F

Date . . .

Listen and repeat **E e** and **F f.** 12 / Unit 3

E  E 

e  e 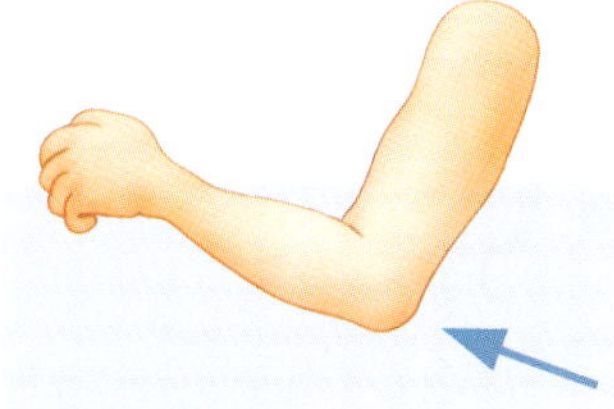

F  F 

f  f 

3. Write

Trace and write **E** and **e**.

Listen and write the beginning letter. MP3 **13** / Unit 3

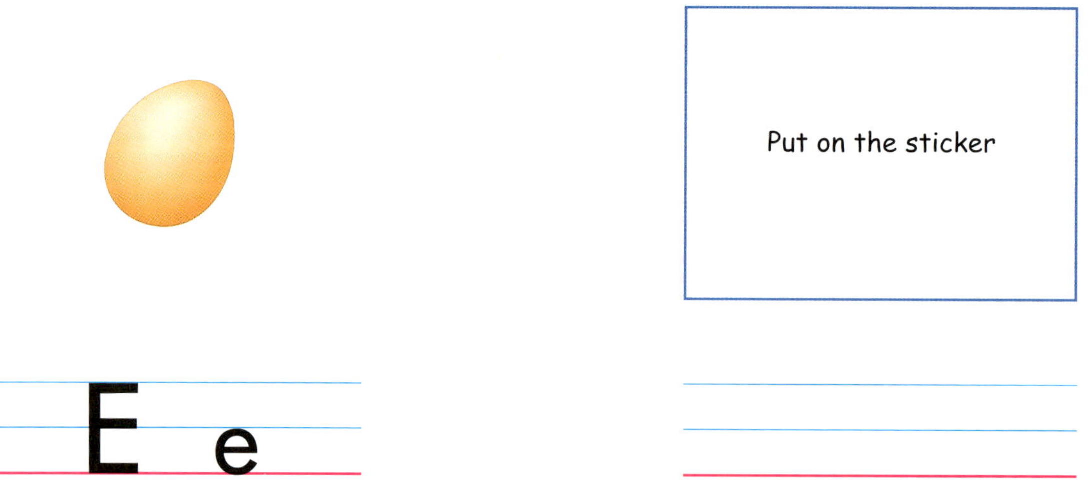

Date . . .

Trace and write **F** and **f**.

Listen and write the beginning letter.

MP3 **14** / Unit 3

Put on the sticker

F f

4. Speak

Say the beginning letters.
Put on the stickers.

1

2

5. Remember

Circle the letters.

E	F	E	B	M	E	E	H
e	e	c	o	e	g	f	e
F	F	R	F	F	T	E	b
f	l	i	f	g	f	k	f

Date . . .

e is for

e is for

E is for

Ee e

f is for

f is for

F is for

Ff f

A B C D E F

PP1-R-1
MP3

Listen and repeat. Circle the animals.  **16** / Review 1

Date . . .

Activity 2

 Listen and count the beginning letters.  17 / Review 1

A a 2 ______ B b ______ C c ______

D d ______ E e ______ F f ______

  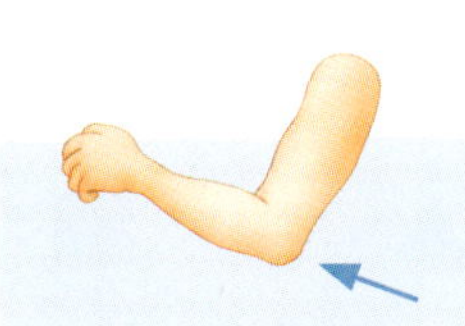 

Activity 3

Fill in the blanks.

A a	B b	C c	D d	E e	F f
▲	■	♣	♤	♡	☆

1 B e e

■ ♡ ♡

2 ___ ___ ___

♤ ▲ ♤

3 ___ ___ ___

Date . . .

Listen and write the letters.

Capital letters	Small letters
1 B	______ 1
2 ______	______ 2
3 ______	______ 3
4 ______	______ 4
5 ______	______ 5
6 ______	______ 6

Score ______

G g H h

PP1-04
MP3

Let's sing G g and H h. MP3 19 / Unit 4

G and H

Date . . .

2. Listen

 Listen and repeat **G g** and **H h.** MP3 **20** / / Unit 4

G  G 

g  g 

H  H 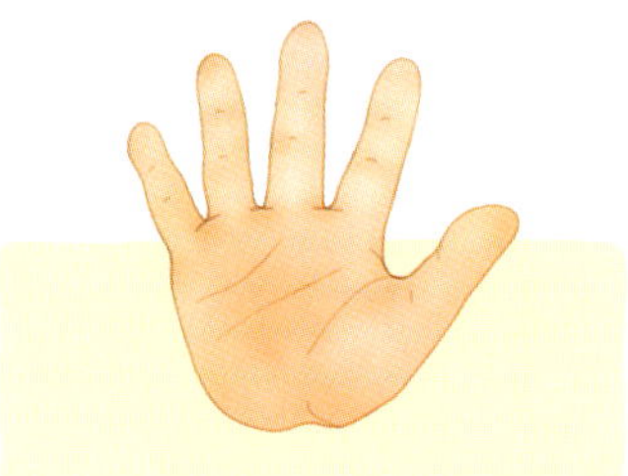

h  h 

3. Write

Trace and write **G** and **g**.

G g

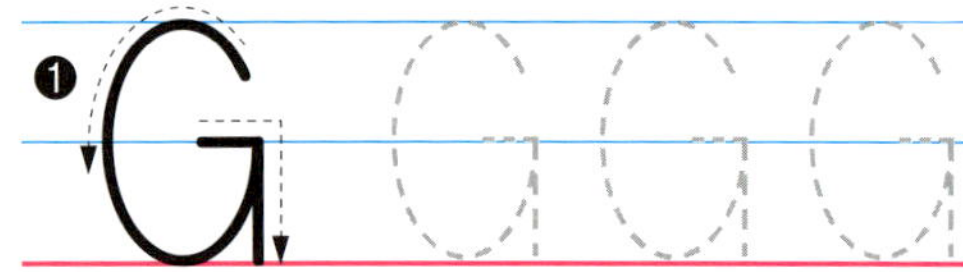

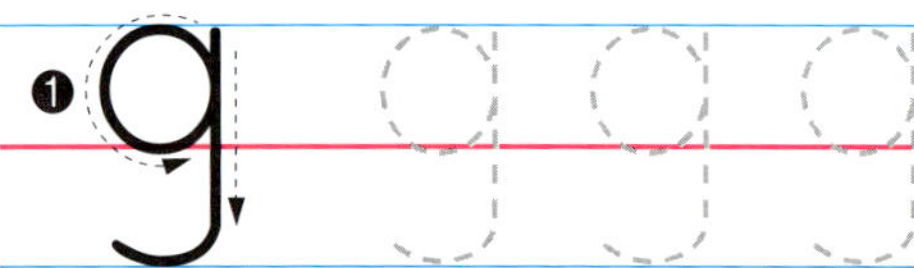

Trace and write **H** and **h**.

H h

 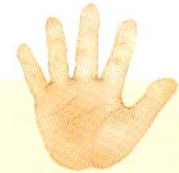  

Date . . .

Listen and circle the beginning letter. MP3 21 / Unit 4

1

Gg Hh

2

Gg Hh

3

Gg Hh

4

Gg Hh

5

Gg Hh

6

Gg Hh

4. Speak

Say the beginning letters.
Put on the stickers.

1

2

5. Remember

Listen and color the letters. MP3 22 / Unit 4

1 G H

2 G H

3 g h

4 g h

Date . . .

6. Chant

Let's chant G g and H h. MP3 23 / Unit 4

g is for

g is for

G is for

Gg g

h is for

h is for

H is for  

Hh h

I i J j

Let's sing **I i** and **J j**. MP3 **24** / Unit 5

I and J

Date . . .

2. Listen

Listen and repeat **I i** and **J j**. MP3 25 / Unit 5

I  I 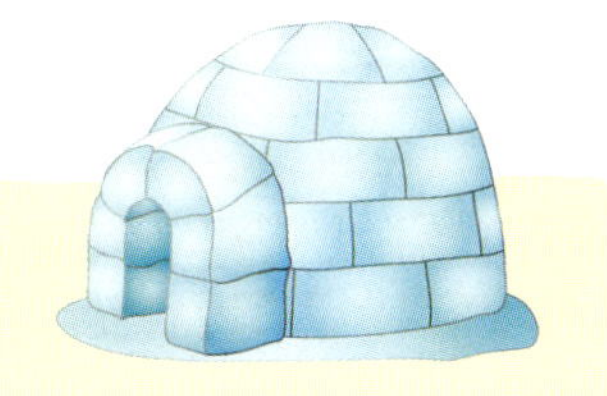

i  i 

J  J 

j  j 

3. Write

Trace and write **I** and **i**.

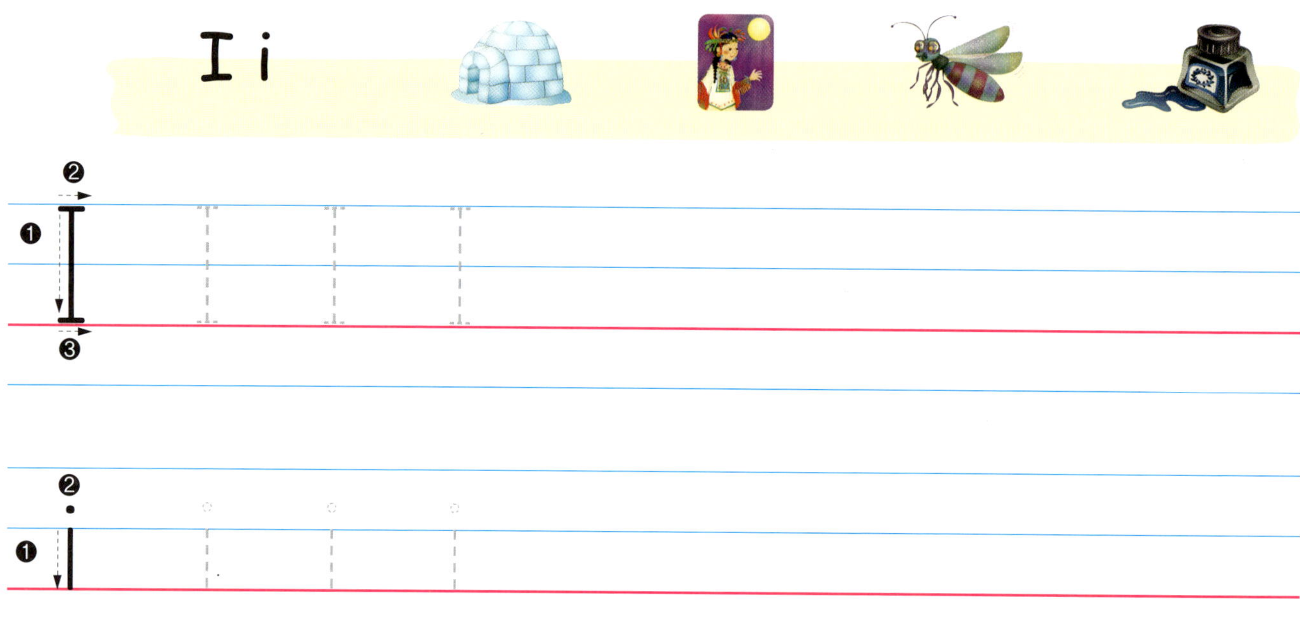

Trace and write **J** and **j**.

Date . . .

Listen and circle the beginning letter.

26 / Unit 5

1

Ii Jj

2

Ii Jj

3

Ii Jj

4

Ii Jj

5

Ii Jj

6

Ii Jj

4. Speak

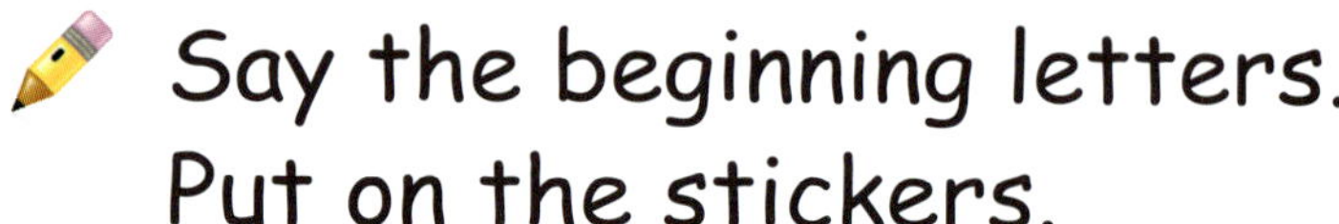

Say the beginning letters.
Put on the stickers.

1

2

5. Remember

Listen and color the letters. MP3 **27** / Unit 5

1 I J

2

3

4

Date . . .

6. Chant

Let's chant I i and J j. MP3 28 / Unit 5

i is for 

i is for 

I is for  

Ii i

j is for 

j is for 

J is for 

Jj j

K k L l

PP1-06
MP3

Let's sing **K k** and **L l**. MP3 **29** / Unit 6

K and L

Date . . .

2. Listen

Listen and repeat **K k** and **L l**. MP3 **30** / Unit 6

K  K 

k  k 

L  L 

l  l 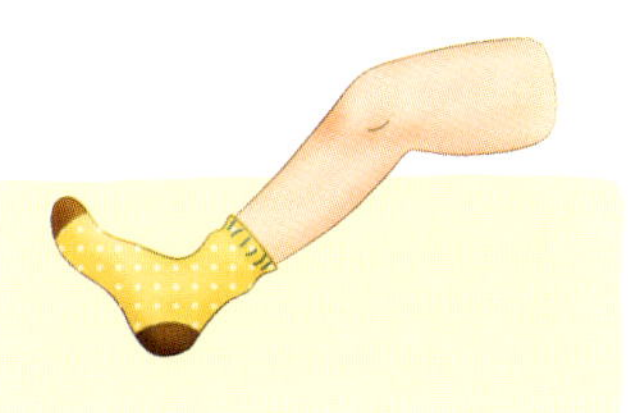

3. Write

Trace and write **K** and **k**.

Trace and write **L** and **l**.

Kl

Date . . .

Listen and circle the beginning letter. MP3 31 / Unit 6

1

Kk Ll

2

Kk Ll

3

Kk Ll

4

Kk Ll

5

Kk Ll

6

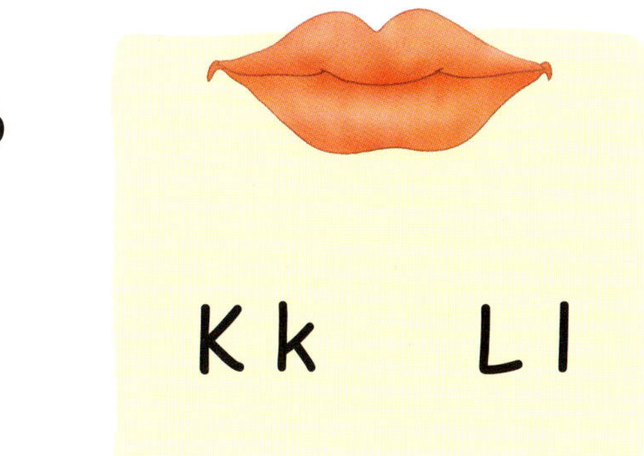

Kk Ll

4. Speak

Say the beginning letters.
Put on the stickers.

1

2

5. Remember

Listen and color the letters. MP3 32 / Unit 6

1 K L

2 K L

3 k l

4 k l

Date . . .

6. Chant

Let's chant K k and L l. MP3 33 / Unit 6

k is for

k is for 

K is for  

Kk k

l is for

l is for

L is for  

Ll l

G H I J K L

MP3

Listen and repeat. Circle the people. .MP3 34 / Review 2

Date . . .

Activity 2

Listen and circle the pictures with the correct beginning letters. .MP3 35 / Review 2

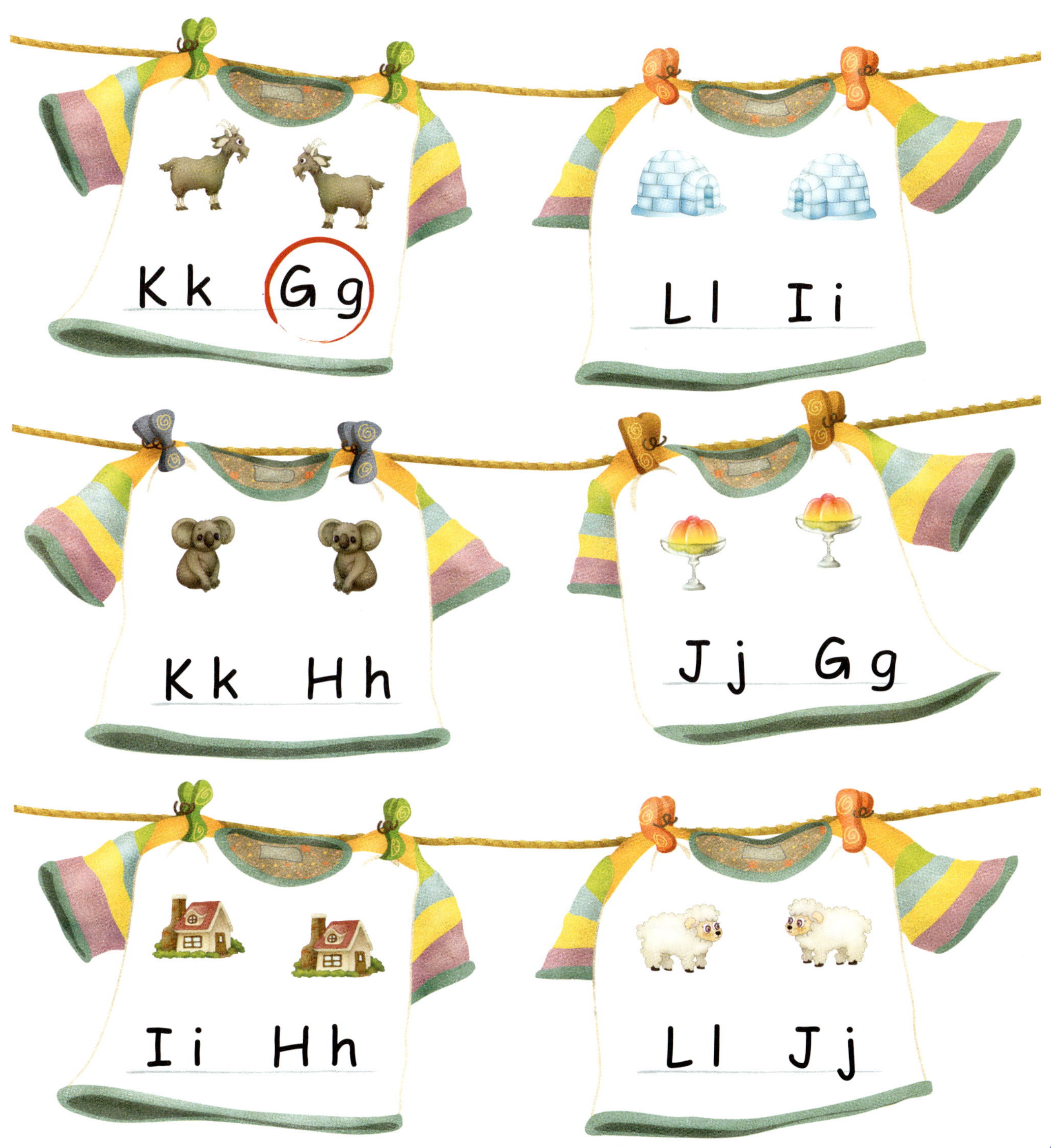

Activity 3

Color the picture.

Gg (green)	Hh (orange)	Ii (red-orange)	Jj (yellow)	Kk (purple)	Ll (blue)

Date . . .

Listen and write the letters. MP3 36 / Review 2

Capital letters

Capital letters	Small letters
1 ______	______ 1
2 ______	______ 2
3 ______	______ 3
4 ______	______ 4
5 ______	______ 5
6 ______	______ 6

Score ______

M m N n

PP1-07
MP3

Let's sing **M m** and **N n.** MP3 **37** / Unit 7

M and N

Date . . .

Listen and repeat **M m** and **N n.** .MP3 **38** / Unit 7

M  M 

m  m 

N  N 

n 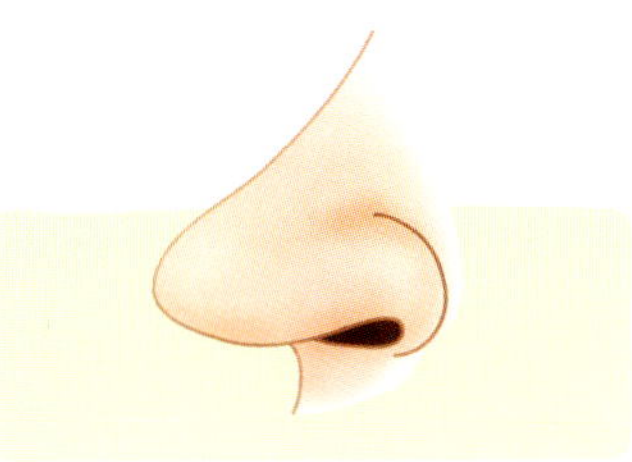 n 

3. Write

Trace and write **M** and **m**.

M m

❶ M ❷ ❸

❶ m ❷

Trace and write **N** and **n**.

N n

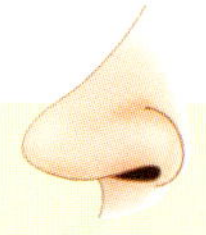

❶ N ❷ ❸

❶ n ❷

Date . . .

Listen and circle the picture that begins with **N n**.

Listen and circle the picture that begins with **M m**.

Listen and circle the picture that begins with **N n**.

4. Speak

Say the beginning letters.
Put on the stickers.

1

2

5. Remember

Listen and circle the letters you hear. MP3 40 / Unit 7

1	m	n	2	n	M
3	M	n	4	N	m
5	N	M	6	m	N

Date . . .

Let's chant **M m** and **N n.** .MP3 41 / Unit 7

m is for 

m is for 

M m is for  

Mm m

n is for 

n is for 

N n is for  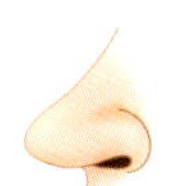

Nn n

O o P p

Let's sing O o and P p. MP3 42 / Unit 8

O and P

Date . . .

2. Listen

o

o

P

P

p

p

3. Write

Trace and write **O** and **o**.

Trace and write **P** and **p**.

Date . . .

 Listen and circle the picture that begins with **O o**.

 44 / Unit 8

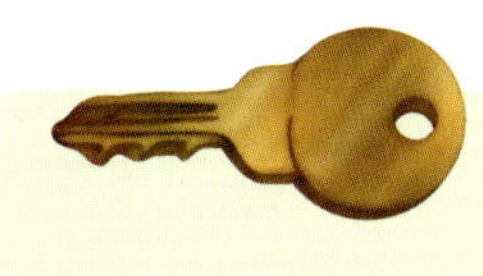   

Listen and circle the picture that begins with **P p**.

Listen and circle the picture that begins with **O o**.

Listen and circle the picture that begins with **P p**.

4. Speak

Say the beginning letters.
Put on the stickers.

1

2

5. Remember

Listen and circle the letters you hear. MP3 45 / Unit 8

1	o	P
2	p	o
3	O	P
4	P	o
5	p	O
6	o	p

Date . . .

Let's chant O o and P p. MP3 46 / Unit 8

o is for 

o is for 

O is for  

Oo o

p is for 

p is for 

P is for  

Pp p

Q q R r

Let's sing **Q q** and **R r.** MP3 **47** / Unit 9

Q and R

Date . . .

2. Listen

 Listen and repeat **Q q** and **R r.** .MP3 **48** / Unit 9

q  q 

R  R 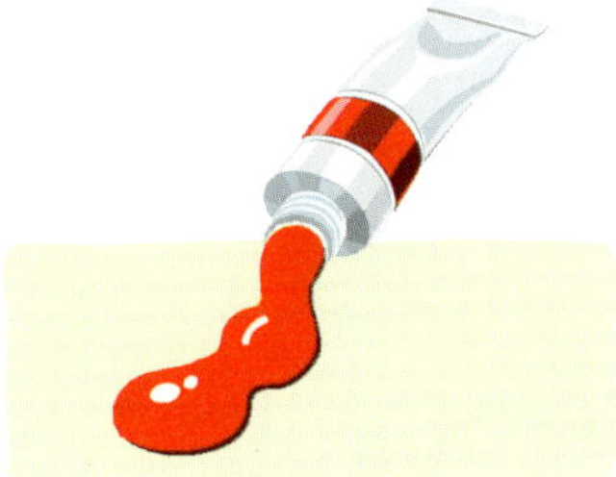

r  r 

3. Write

 Trace and write **Q** and **q**.

Q q

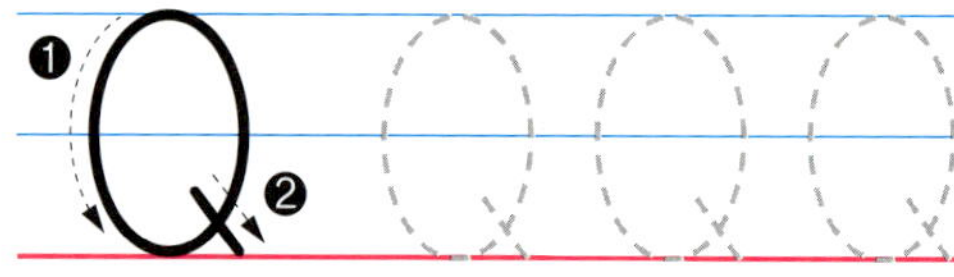

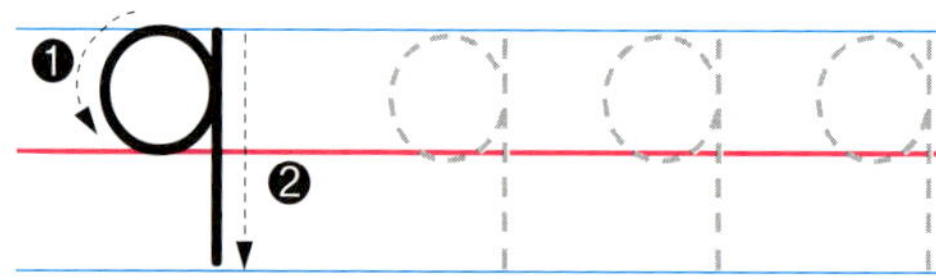

 Trace and write **R** and **r**.

R r

Date . . .

Listen and circle the picture that begins with **Q q**.

MP3 **49** / Unit 9

Listen and circle the picture that begins with **R r**.

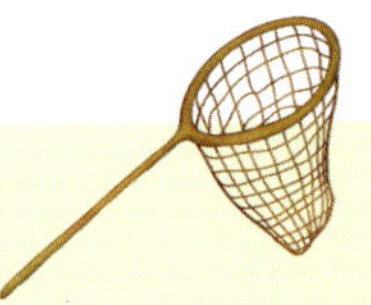

Listen and circle the picture that begins with **Q q**.

Listen and circle the picture that begins with **R r**.

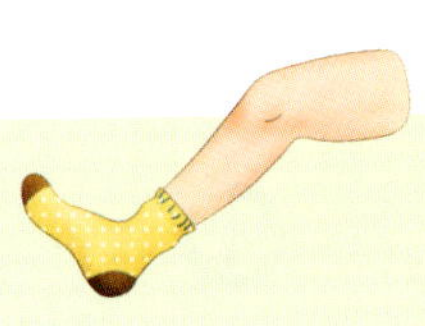

4. Speak

Say the beginning letters.
Put on the stickers.

1

2

5. Remember

Listen and circle the letters you hear. MP3 50 / Unit 9

1	Q	R	2	r	q
3	R	q	4	q	R
5	R	Q	6	q	r

Date . . .

6. Chant

Let's chant Q q and R r. MP3 51 / Unit 9

q is for 

q is for 

Q is for  

Qq q

r is for 

r is for 

R is for 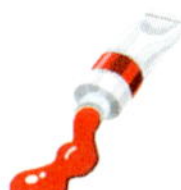 

Rr r

M N O P Q R

PP1-R-3
MP3

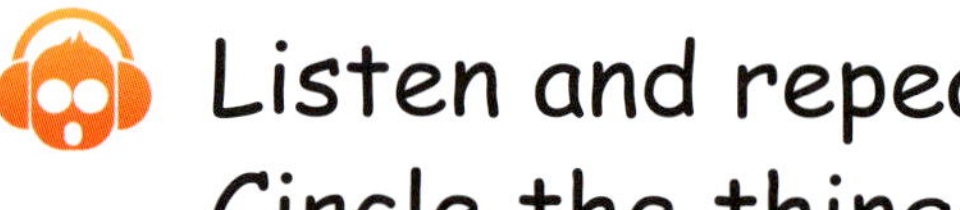

Listen and repeat.
Circle the things that you have.  52 / Review 3

Date . . .

Activity 2

Listen and count the beginning letters. MP3 53 / Review 3

Mm 1	Nn ____	Oo ____
Pp ____	Qq ____	Rr ____

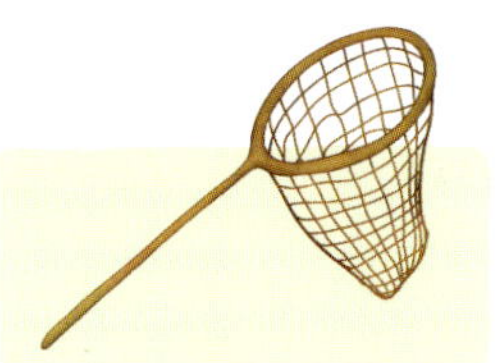

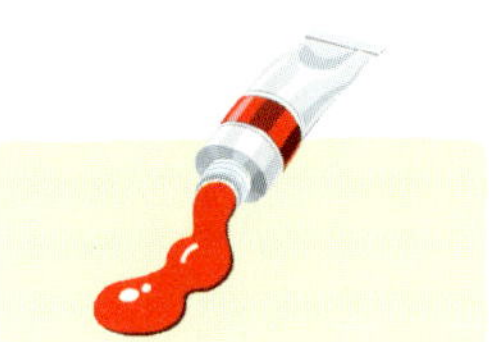

Activity 3

Listen and color the pictures with the correct beginning letters. MP3 54 / Review 3

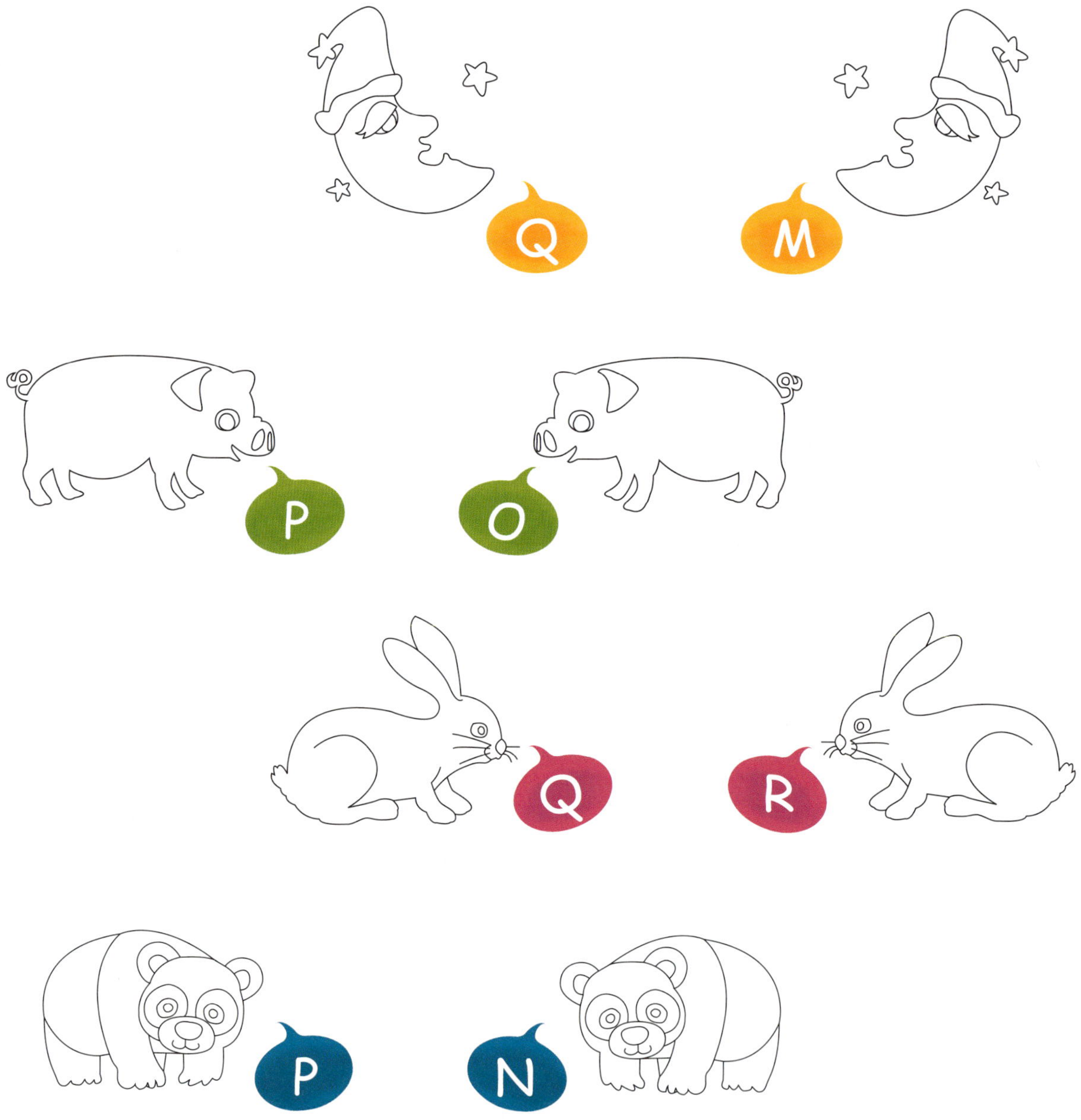

Q M

P O

Q R

P N

Date . . .

Listen and write the letters. MP3 55 / Review 3

Capital letters		Small letters	
1	______	______	1
2	______	______	2
3	______	______	3
4	______	______	4
5	______	______	5
6	______	______	6

Score ______

S s T t

PP1-10
MP3

Let's sing S s and T t. MP3 56 / Unit 10

S and T

Date . . .

Listen and repeat S s and T t. MP3 57 / Unit 10

S 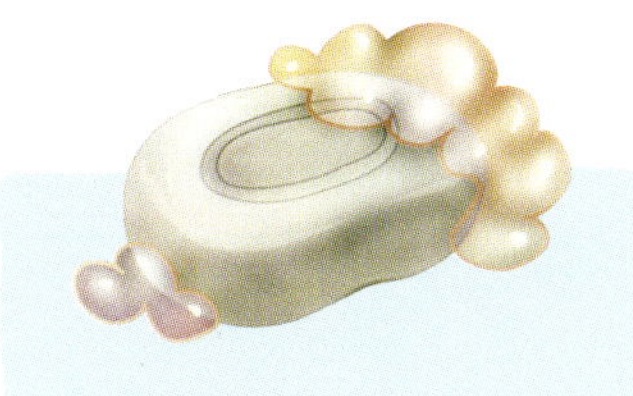 S 

s  s 

T  T 

t  t 

Trace and write **S** and **s**.

S s

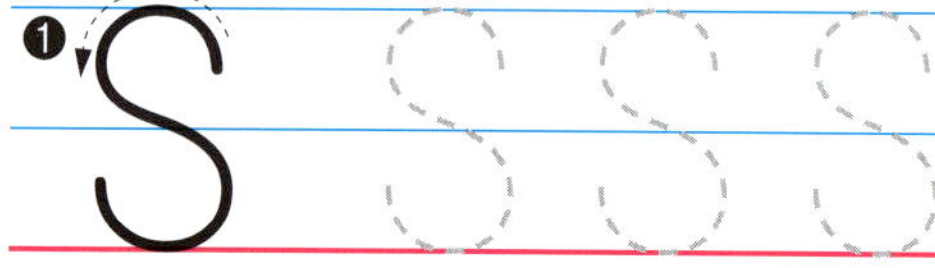

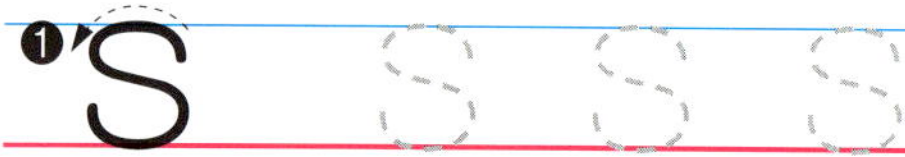

Trace and write **T** and **t**.

T t

Date . . .

Listen and check ✓ the picture that has a different beginning letter.

.MP3 **58** / Unit 10

1

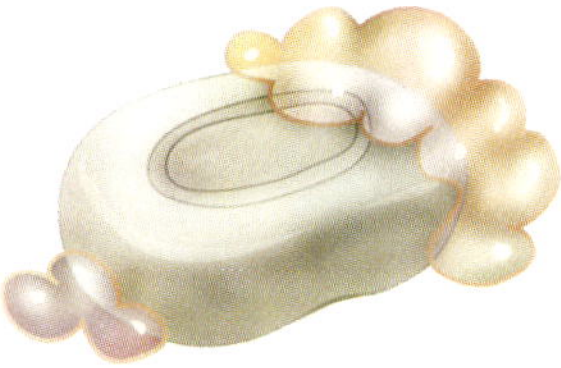

2

3

4. Speak

Say the beginning letters.
Put on the stickers.

5. Remember

Fill in the blanks in '**S T s t**' order.

Date . . .

Let's chant S s and T t. MP3 59 / Unit 10

s is for 

s is for 

S is for  

Ss s

t is for 

t is for 

T is for  

Tt t

Uu Vv Ww

Let's sing **U u**, **V v**, and **W w**. MP3 60 / Unit 11

U, V, and W

U u U U u U U u U It sounds u

V v V V v V V v V It sounds v

W w W W w W W w W It sounds w

This is U This is V This is W U u V v W w

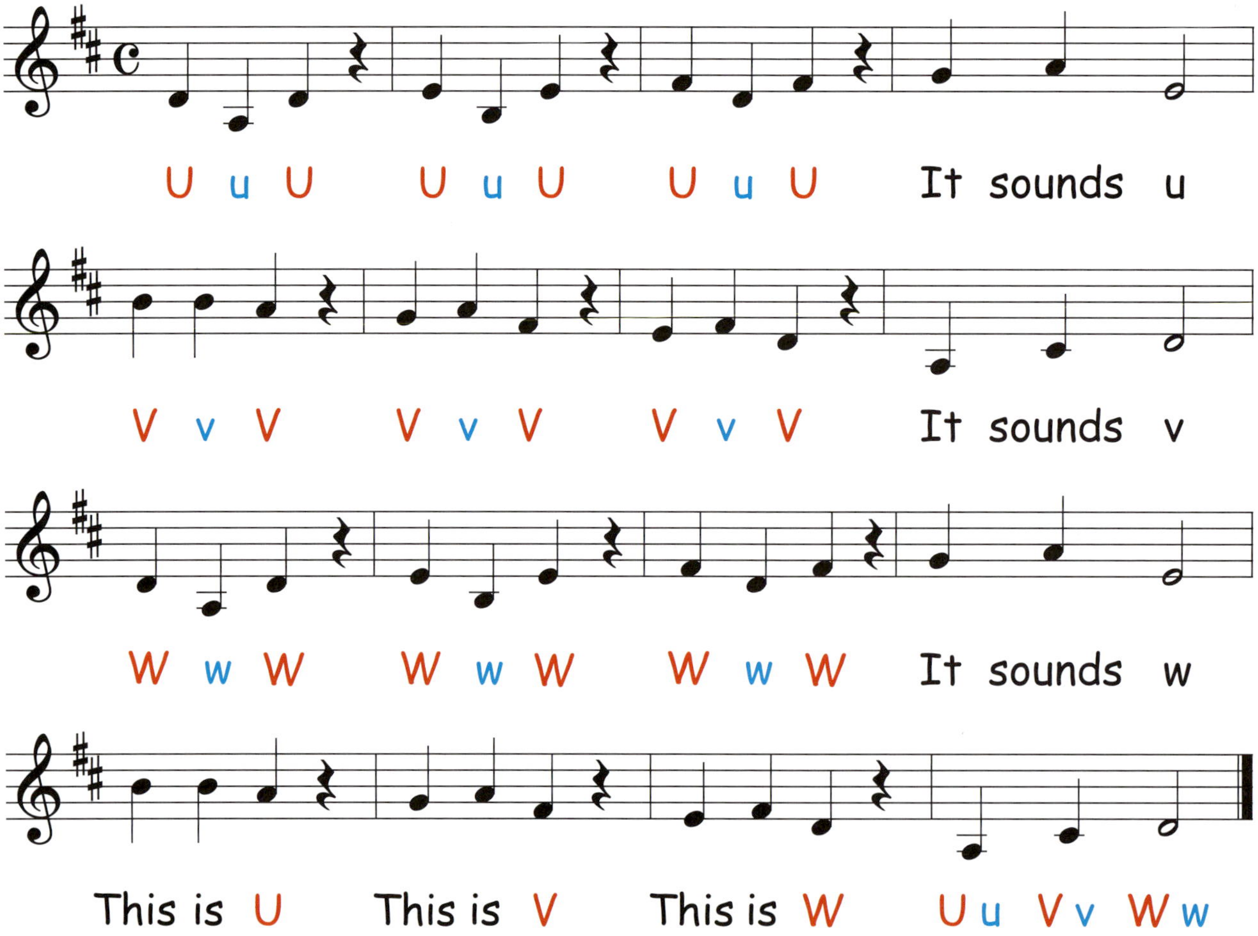

Date . . .

2. Listen

Listen and repeat **U u**, **V v**, and **W w**. MP3 **61** / Unit 11

U u

V v

W w

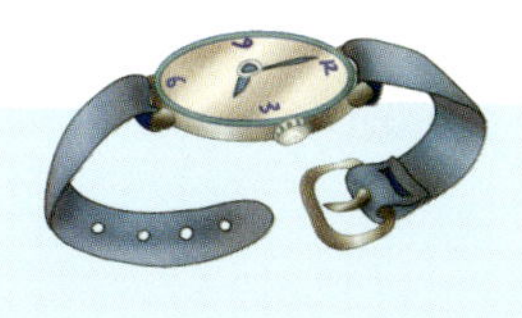

Trace and write **U** and **u**.

U u

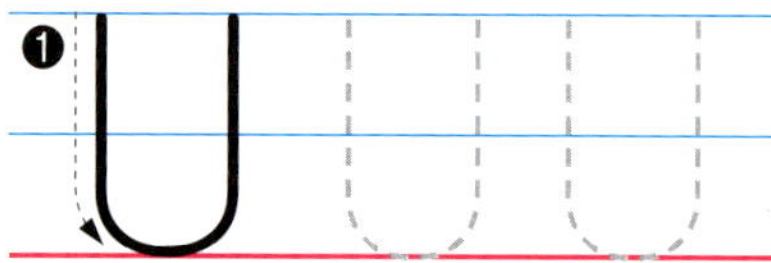
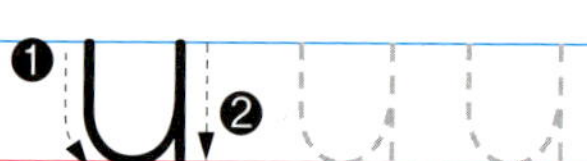

Trace and write **V** and **v**.

V v

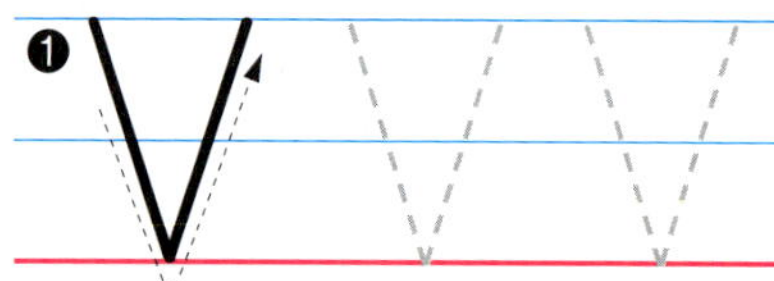

Trace and write **W** and **w**.

W w

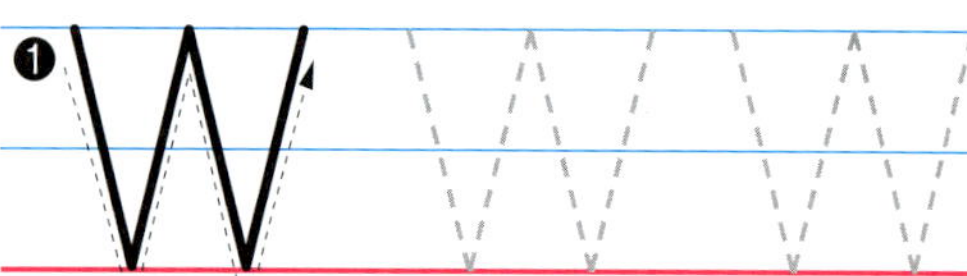

Date . . .

Listen and check the picture that has a different beginning letter. MP3 62 / Unit 11

1

2

3

4. Speak

Say the beginning letters.
Put on the stickers.

1

2

3

5. Remember

Fill in the blanks in '**U V W u v w**' order.

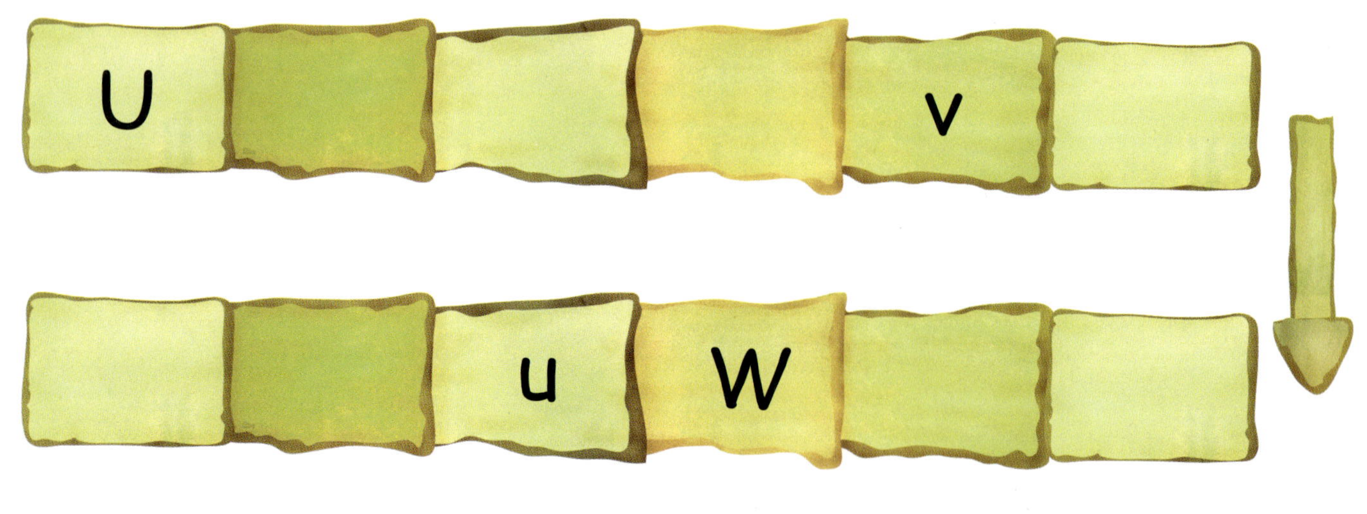

Date . . .

6. Chant

Let's chant **U u**, **V v**, and **W w**. MP3 **63** / Unit 11

U is for

u is for 

V is for 

v is for  

W is for 

w is for  

u v w

Xx Yy Zz

PP1-12
MP3

Let's sing X x, Y y, and Z z. MP3 64 / Unit 12

X, Y, and Z

This - is - X x X x - sounds x x

This - is - Y y Y y - sounds y y

This - is - Z z Z z - sounds z z

Date . . .

2. Listen

 Listen and repeat X x, Y y, and Z z. MP3 **65** / Unit 12

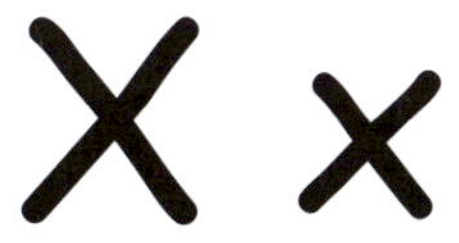

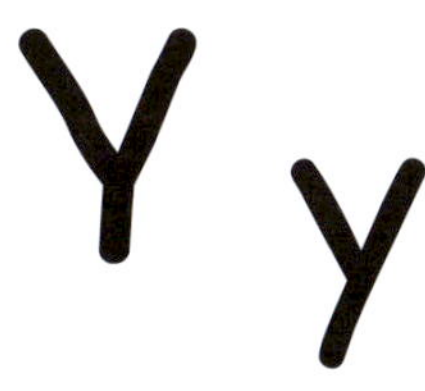

Z z

3. Write

Trace and write **X** and **x**.

X x

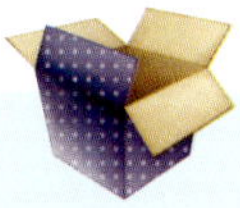
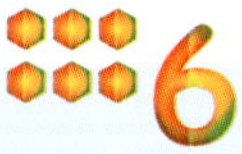
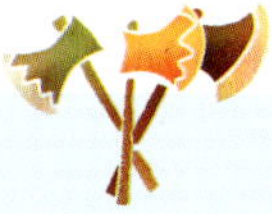

X X X x x x

Trace and write **Y** and **y**.

Y y

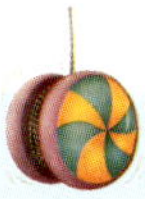
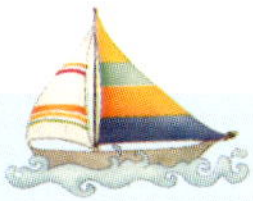
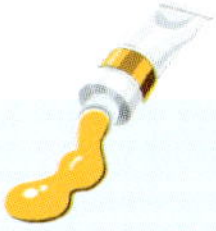

Y Y Y y y y

Trace and write **Z** and **z**.

Z z

Z Z Z z z z

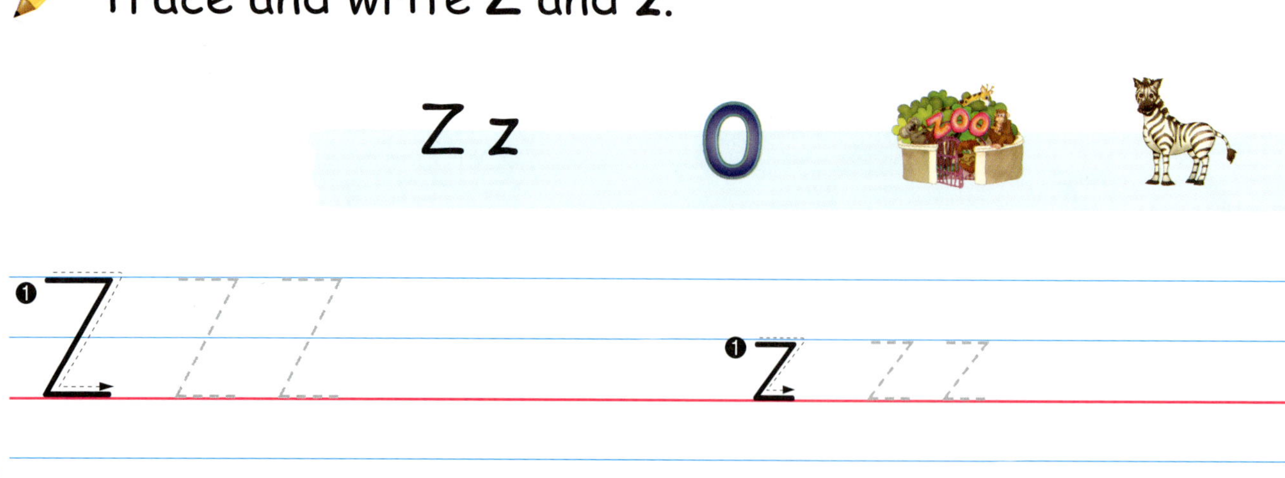

Date . . .

Listen and check ✔ the picture that has a different beginning or ending letter. MP3 66 / Unit 12

1

2

3

4. Speak

Say the beginning letters.
Put on the stickers.

5. Remember

Fill in the blanks in 'X Y Z x y z' order.

Date . . .

X is for

x is for  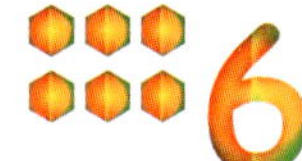

Y is for 

y is for  

Z is for 0

z is for  

x y z

S T U V W X Y Z

PP1-R-4
MP3

Listen and repeat.
Circle the things that are round.

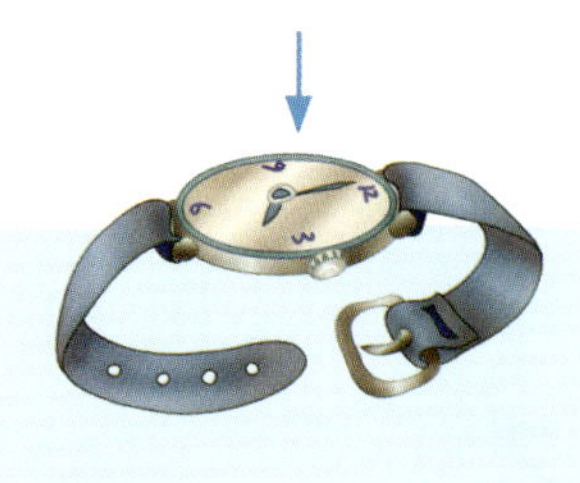

Date . . .

Activity 2

Check if you can read.

Activity 3

Listen and follow the letters you hear. MP3 69 / Review 4

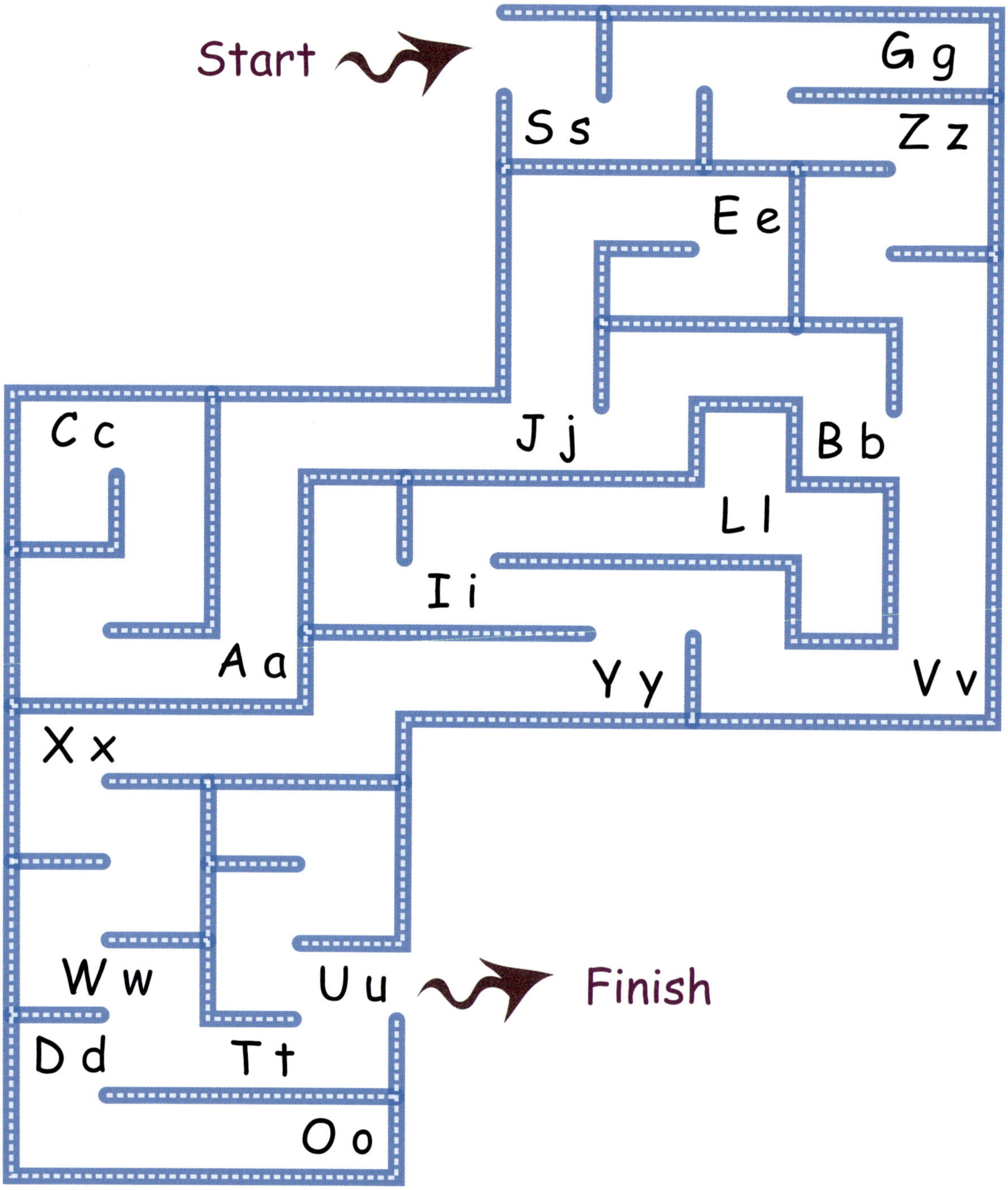

Start

Finish

Date . . .

Listen and write the letters. MP3 70 / Review 4

Capital letters

1 ____
2 ____
3 ____
4 ____
5 ____
6 ____
7 ____
8 ____

____ 1
____ 2
____ 3
____ 4
____ 5
____ 6
____ 7
____ 8

Score ____

Phonics PARTY 1

Unit 1

Unit 2

Unit 3

Unit 4

Unit 5

Unit 6

Unit 7

Unit 8

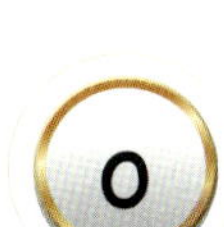

Unit 9

Unit 10

Unit 11

Unit 12

Phonics PARTY

Single Letter Sounds

Workbook

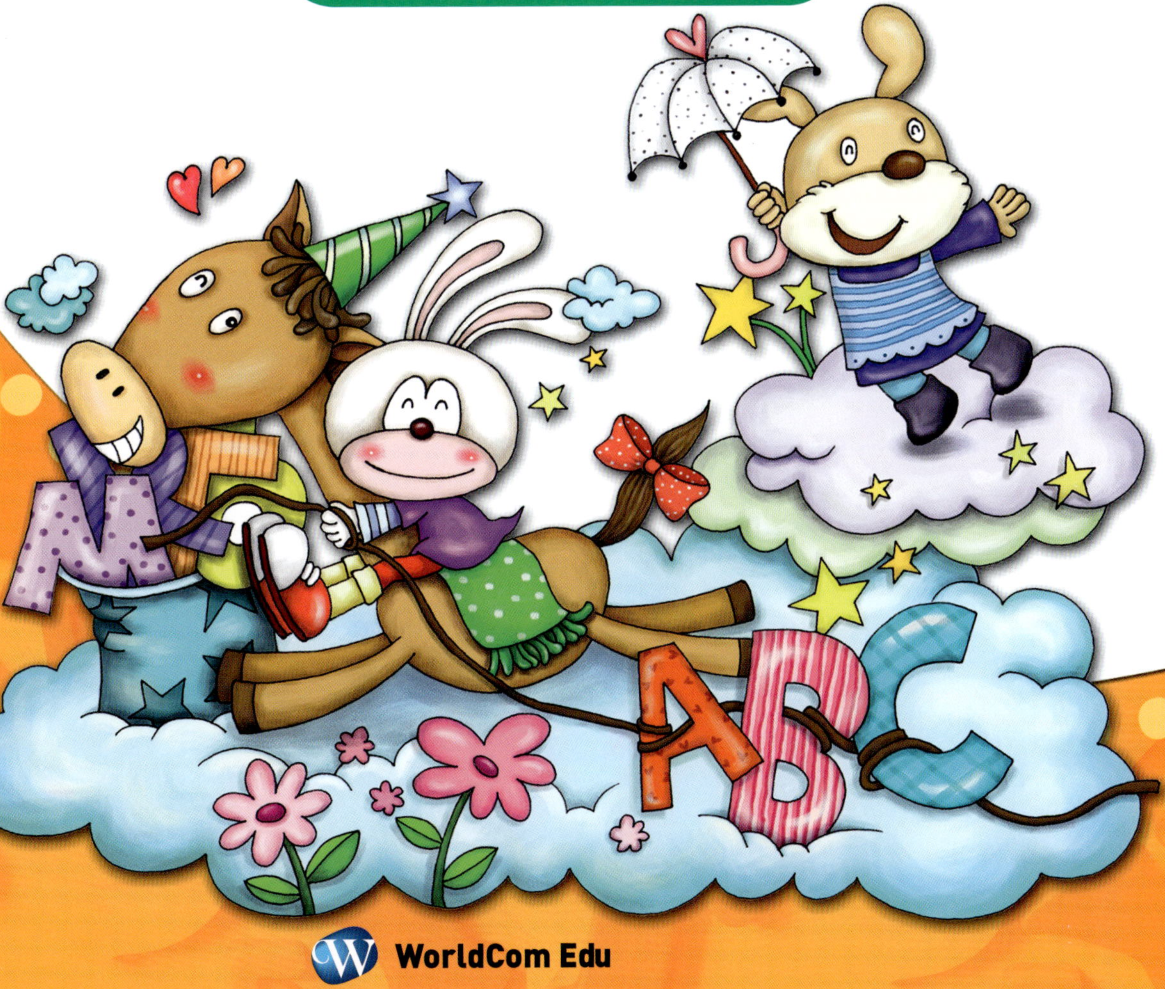

Workbook

A a B b

Ⓐ Trace and write.

A a

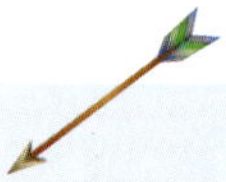

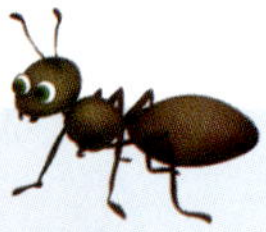

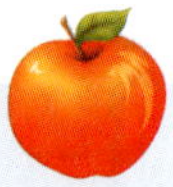

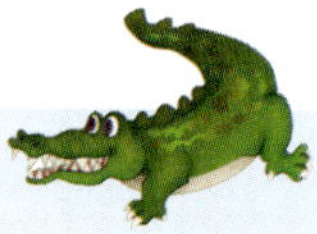

A A A A

a a a a

B b

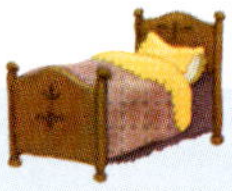

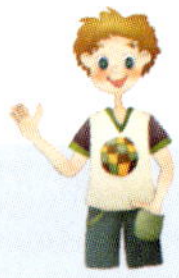

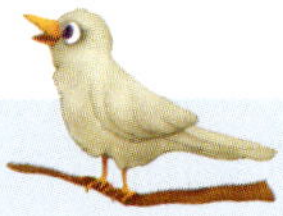

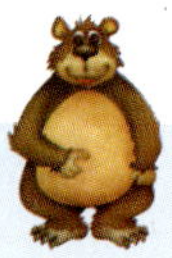

B B B B

b b b b

B Color the right pairs.

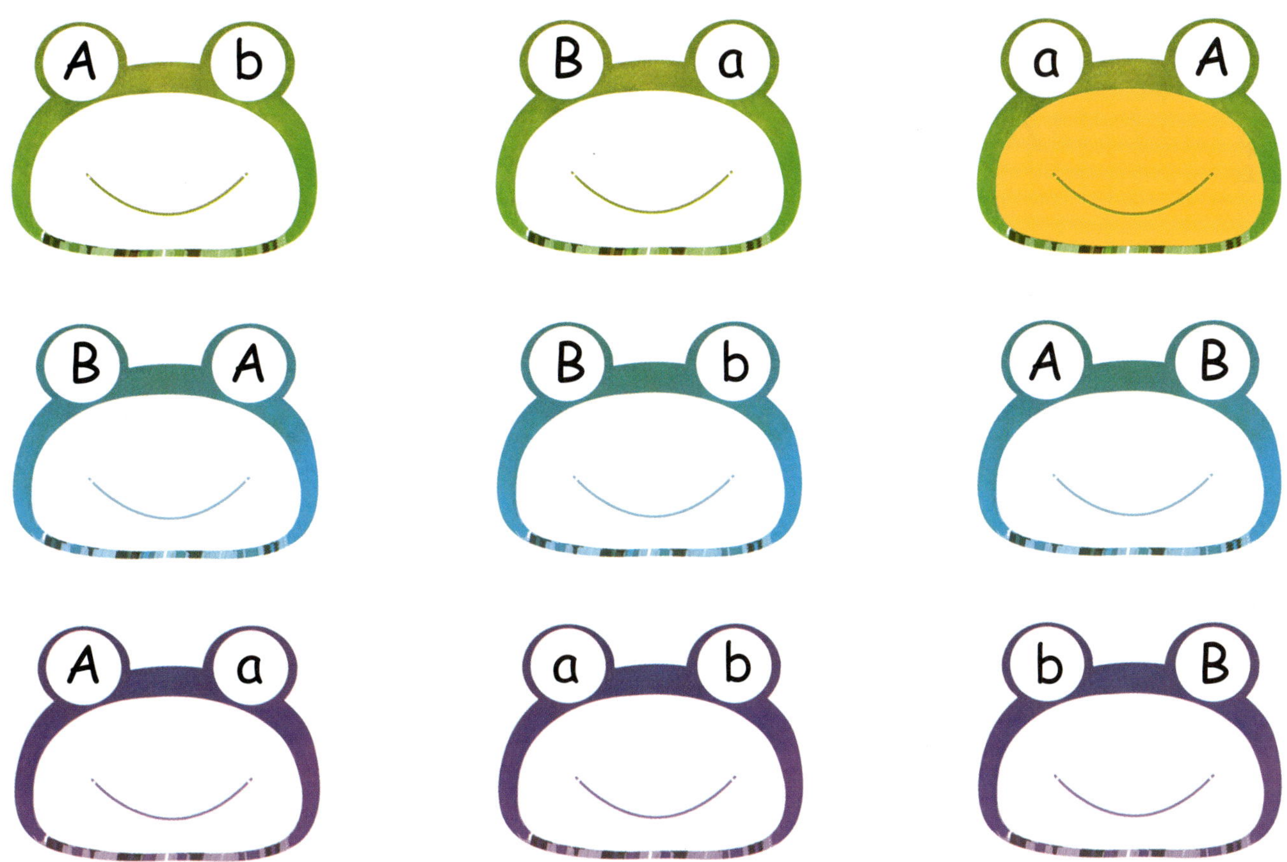

C Circle the right beginning letters for the pictures.

D Check the picture with the right beginning letter.

1

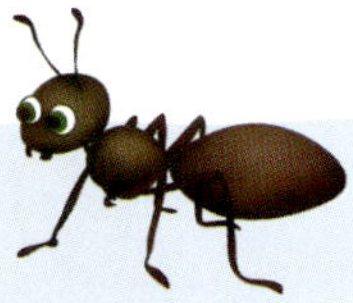

B b	B b	A a
○	✔	○

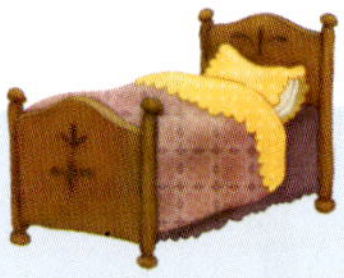

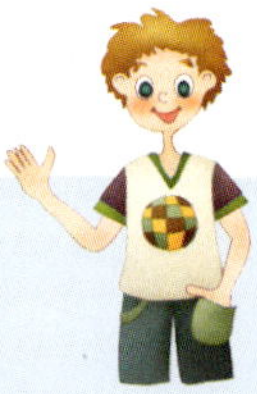

2

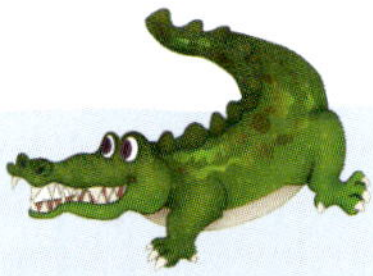

B b	A a	A a
○	○	○

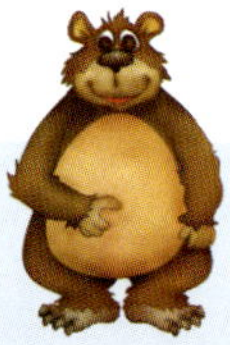

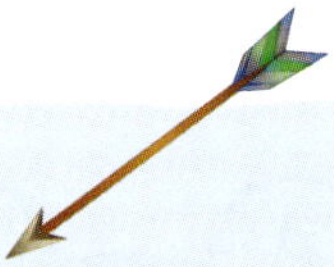

E Match the picture to the beginning letter.

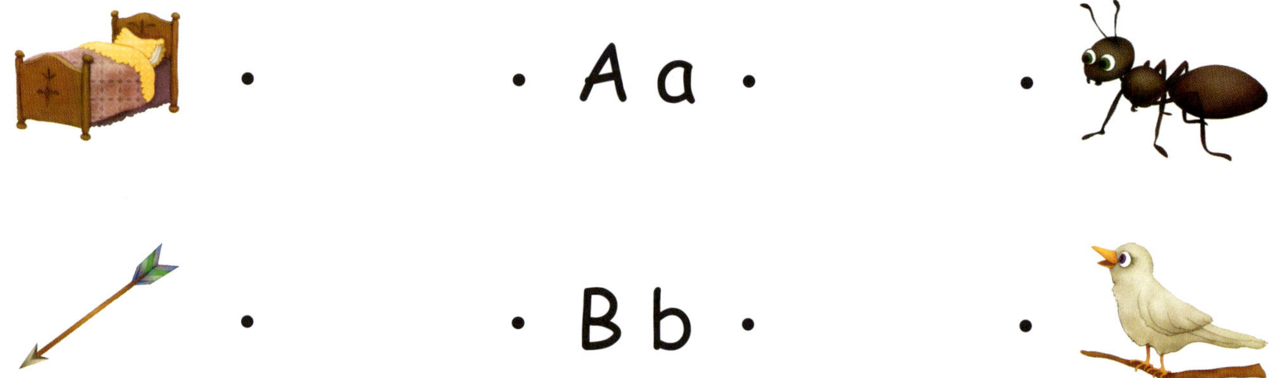

F Write the beginning letter.
Circle the picture with the same beginning letter.

G Say the beginning letters and color the pictures.

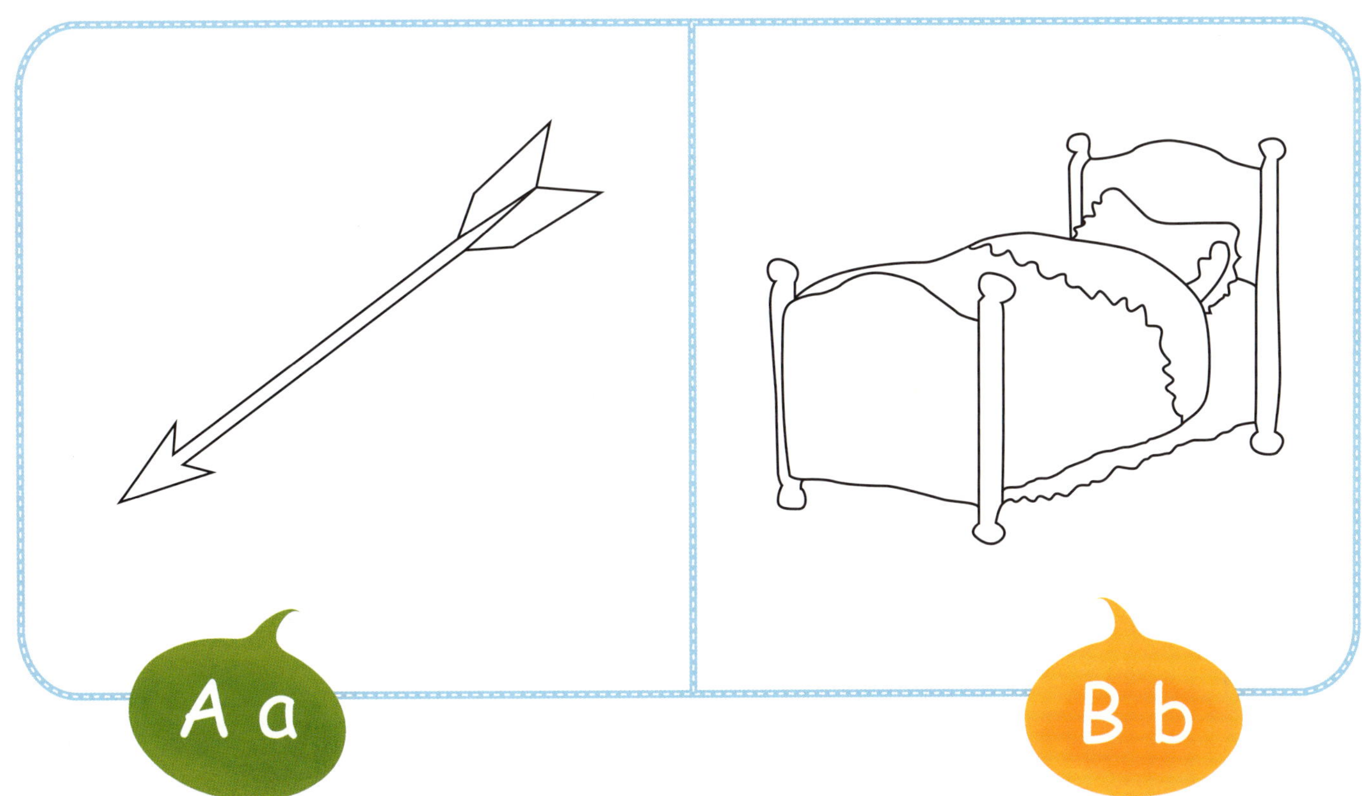

C c D d

Ⓐ Trace and write.

B Color the right pairs.

D c	C c	d c
c d	D C	D d
c C	C D	d D

C Circle the right beginning letters for the pictures.

1 c d

2 c d

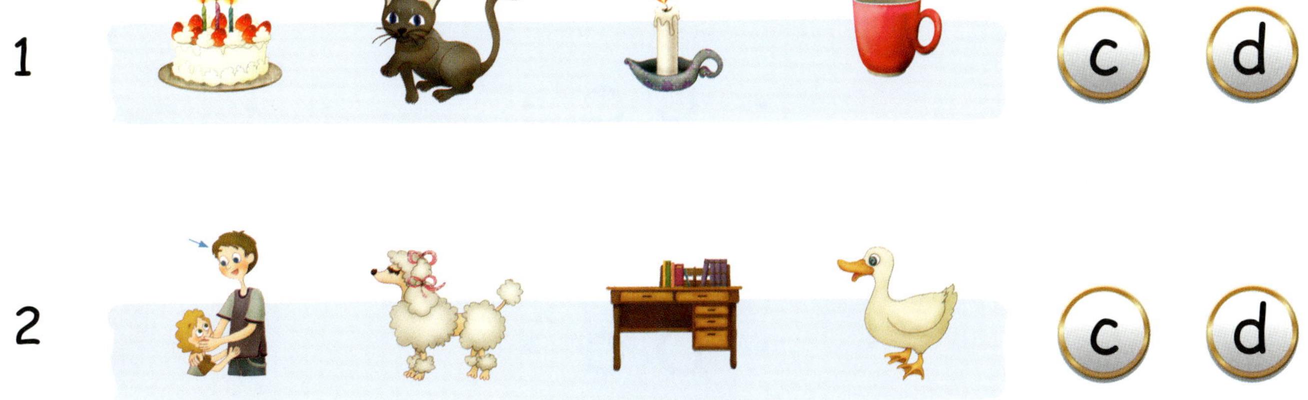

D Check ✓ the picture with the right beginning letter.

1

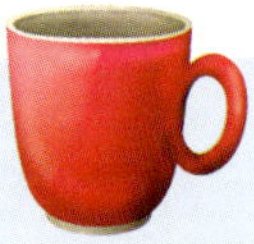

C c

D d

C c

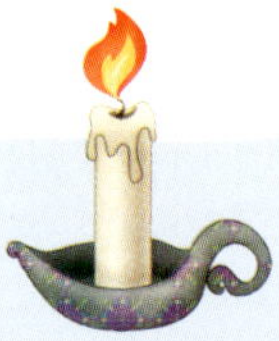

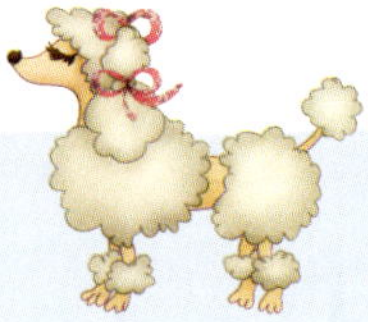

2

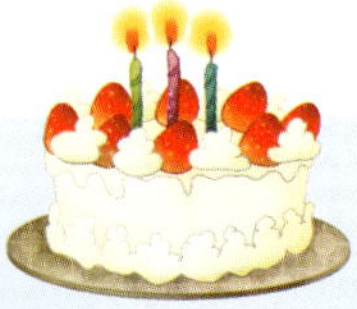

D d

D d

C c

E Match the picture to the beginning letter.

 · · C c · ·

 · · D d · ·

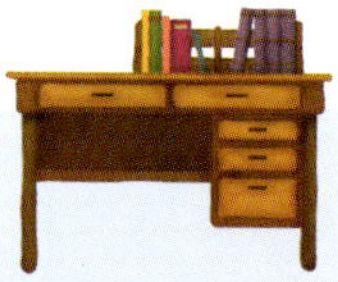

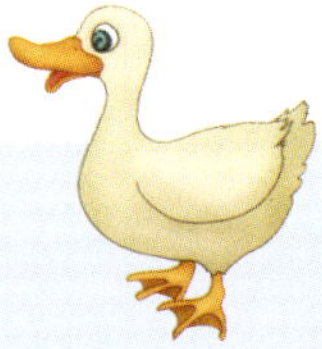

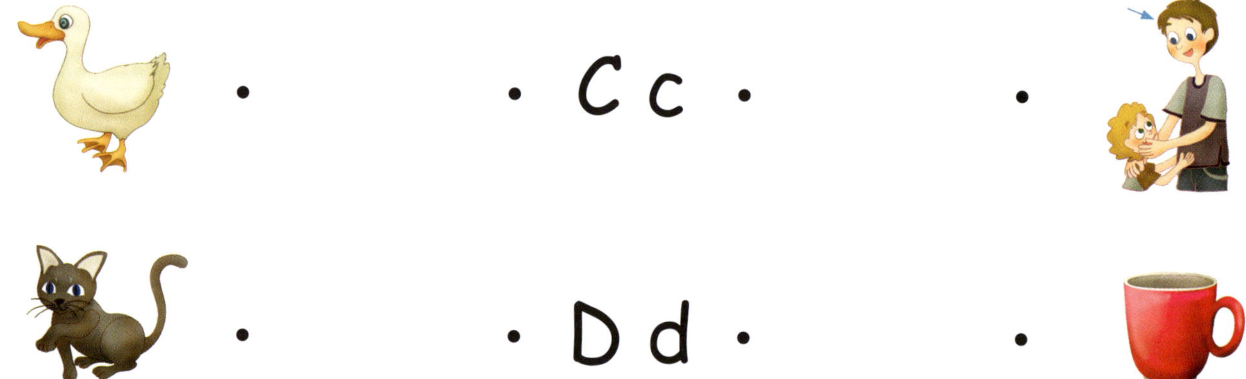

F Write the beginning letter.
Circle the picture with the same beginning letter.

1 ______

2 ______

G Say the beginning letters and color the pictures.

E e F f

Ⓐ Trace and write.

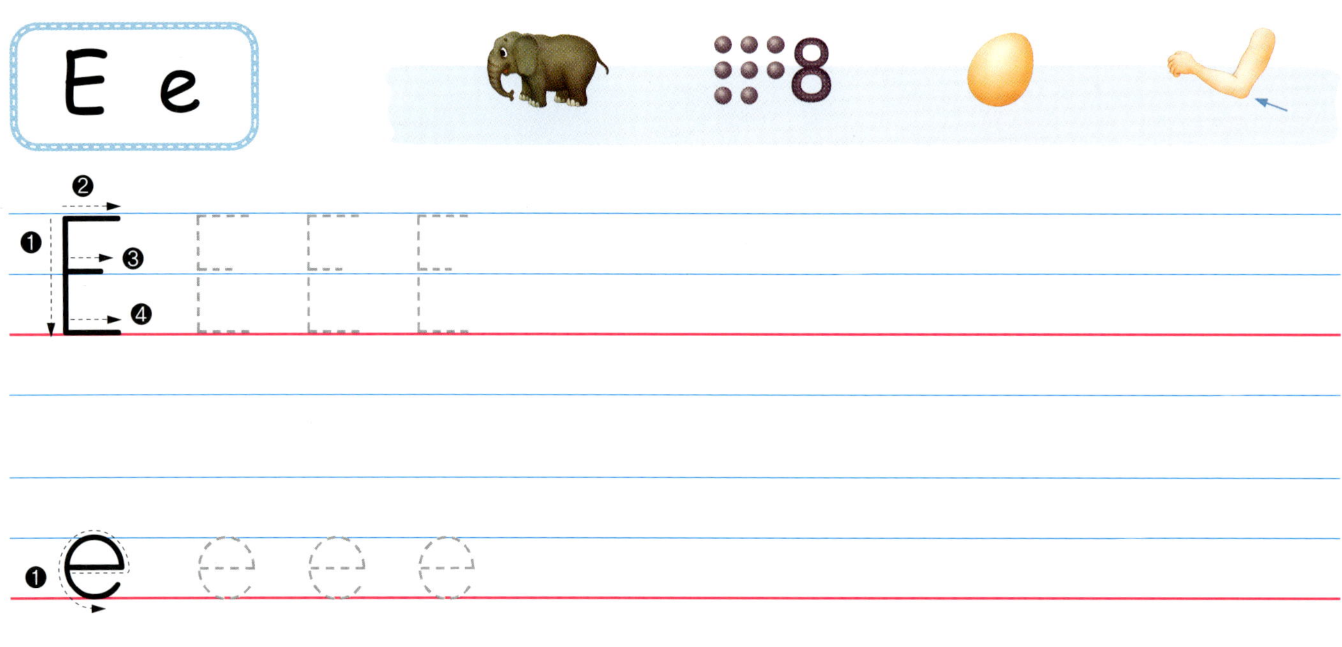

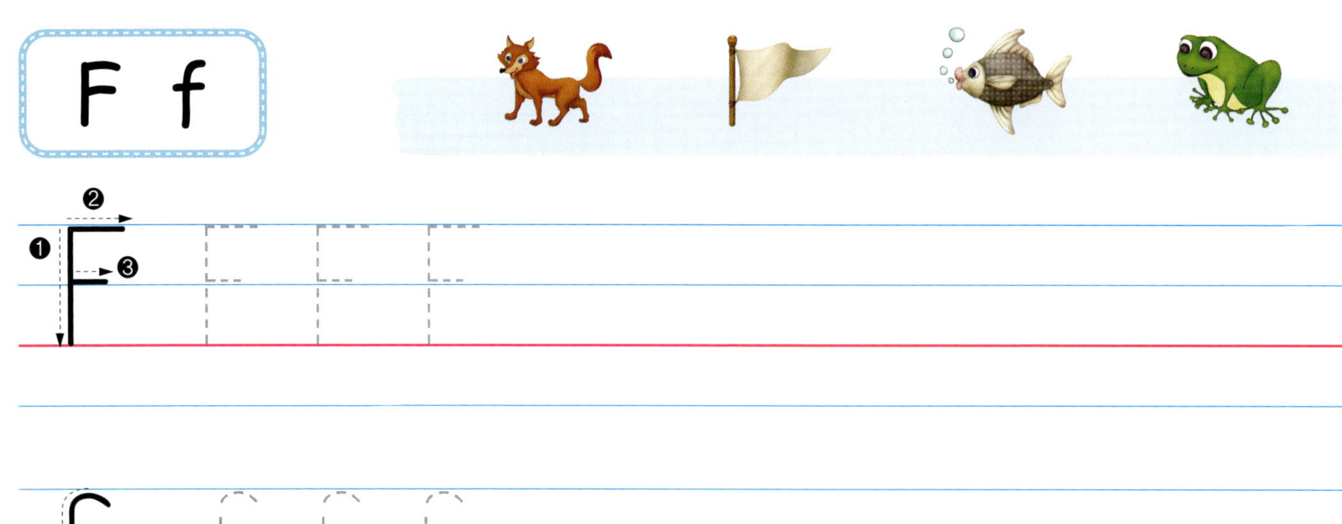

B Color the right pairs.

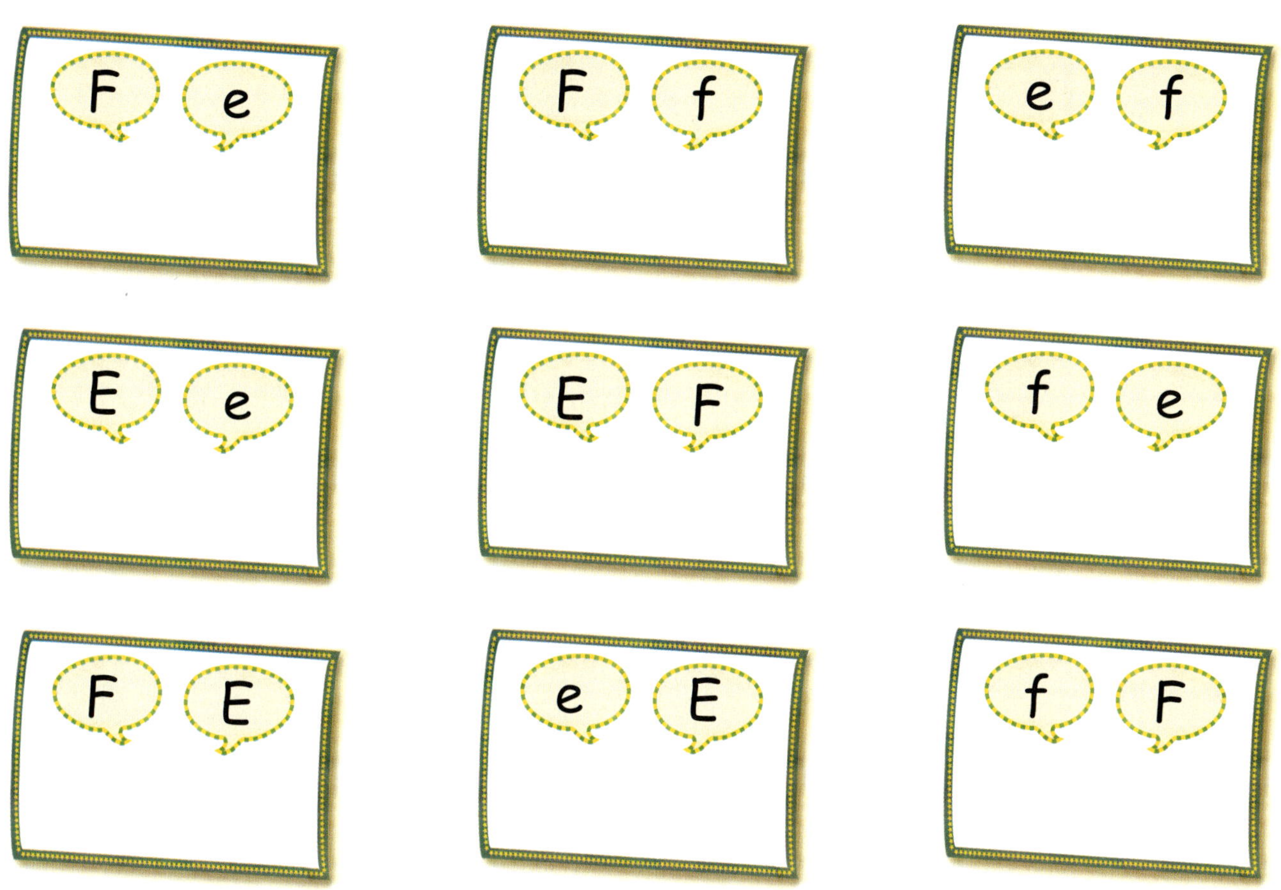

C Circle the right beginning letters for the pictures.

D Check ✔ the picture with the right beginning letter.

1

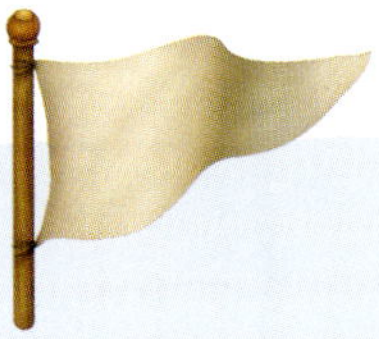

F f	E e	F f
○	○	○

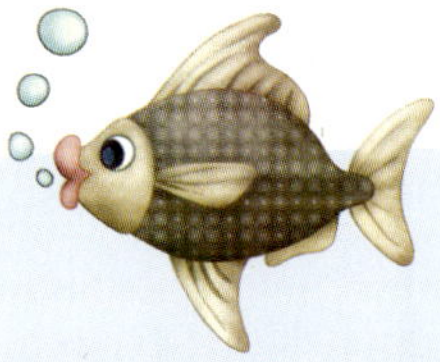

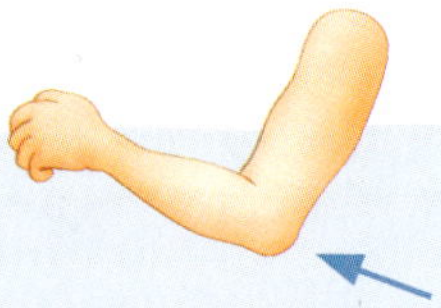

2

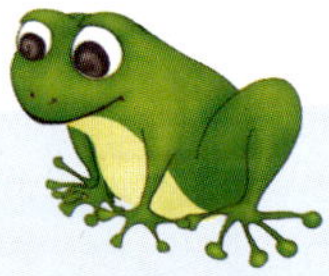

E e	E e	F f
○	○	○

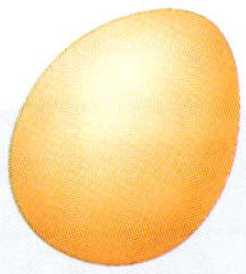

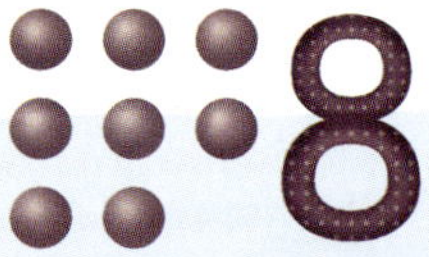

E Match the picture to the beginning letter.

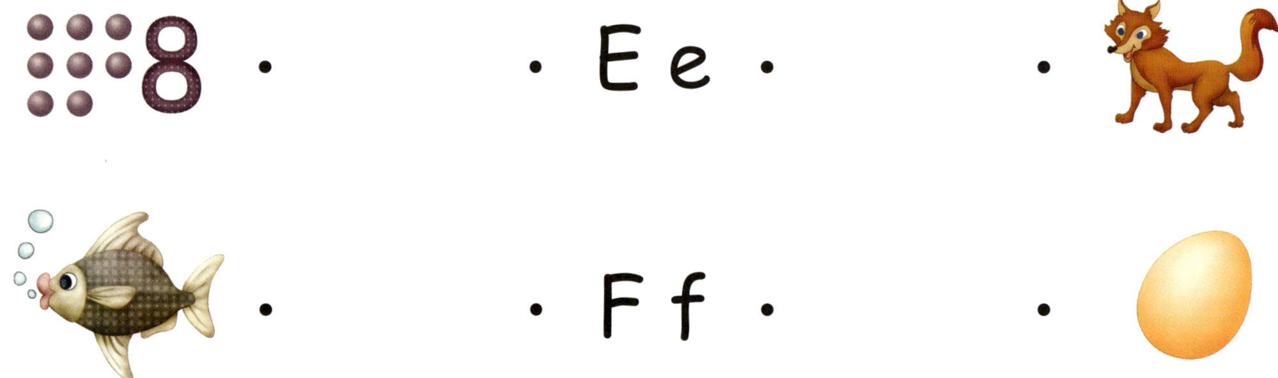

F Write the beginning letter.
Circle the picture with the same beginning letter.

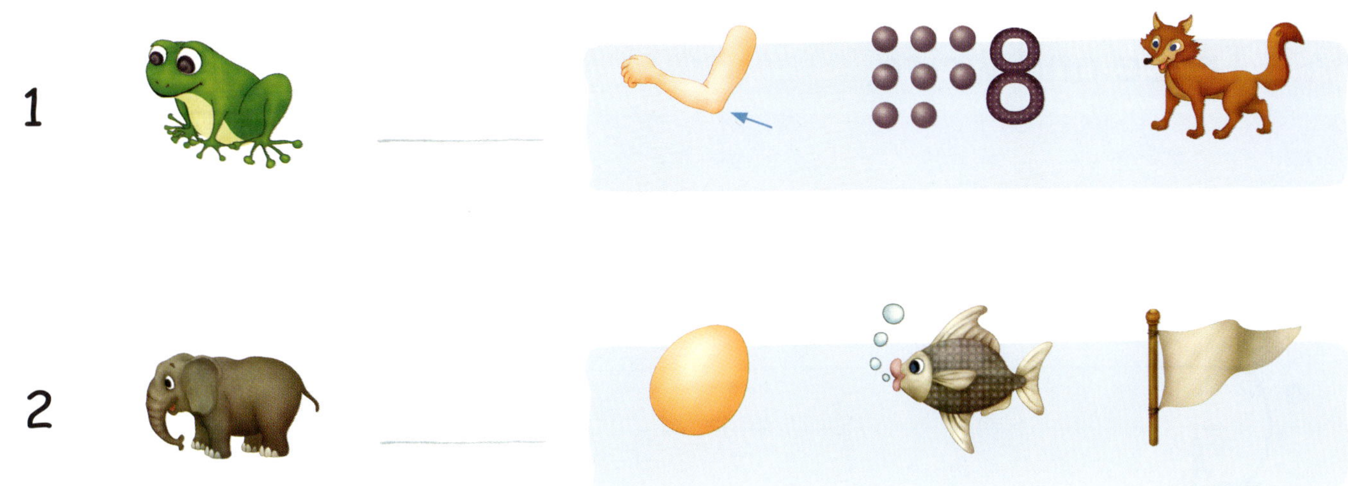

G Say the beginning letters and color the pictures.

G g H h

Ⓐ Trace and write.

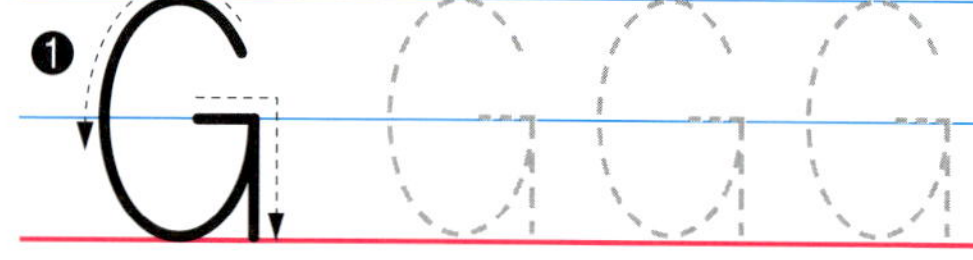

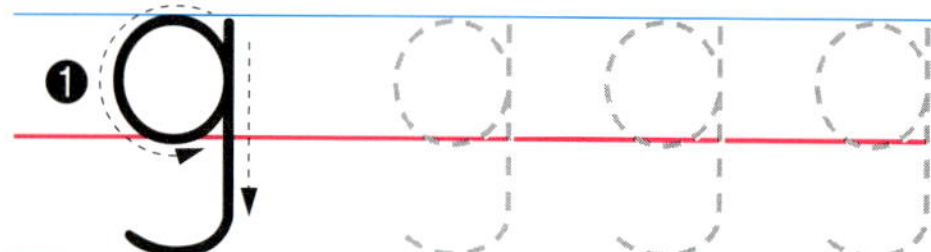

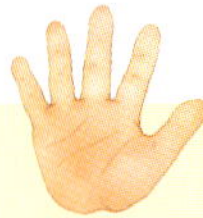

B Color the right pairs.

C Circle the right beginning letters for the pictures.

D Check ✓ the picture with the right beginning letter.

1

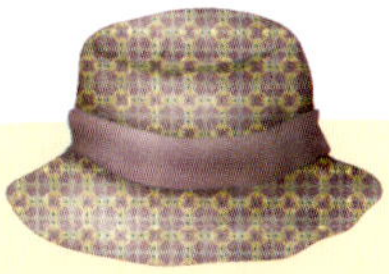

G g ○

G g ○

H h ○

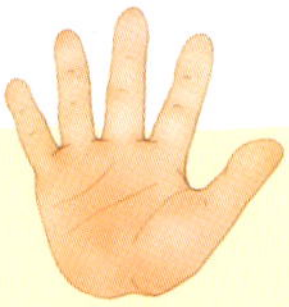

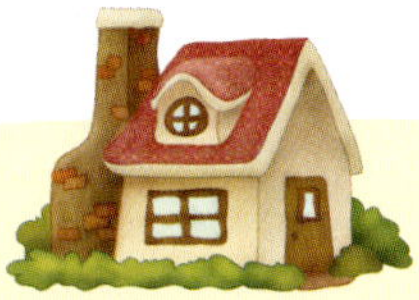

2

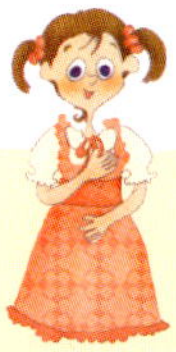

G g ○

H h ○

H h ○

E Match the picture to the beginning letter.

 • • G g • •

 • • H h • •

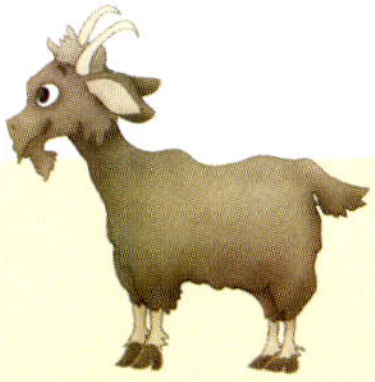

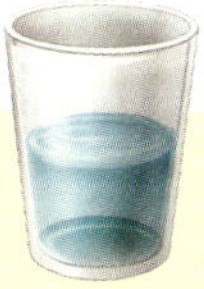

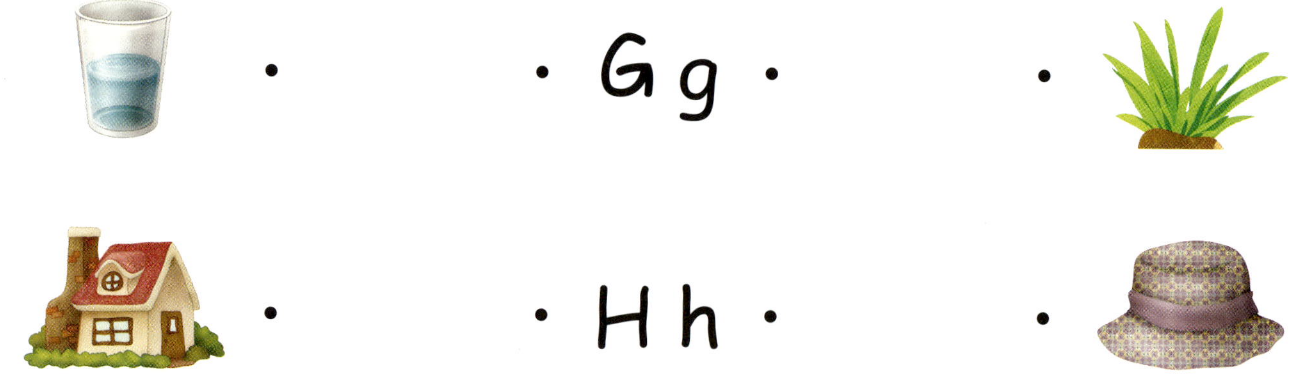

F Write the beginning letter.
Circle the picture with the same beginning letter.

G Say the beginning letters and color the pictures.

I i J j

Ⓐ Trace and write.

I i

❶ ❷ ❸ I

❶ ❷ i

J j

❶ ❷ J

❶ ❷ j

B Color the right pairs.

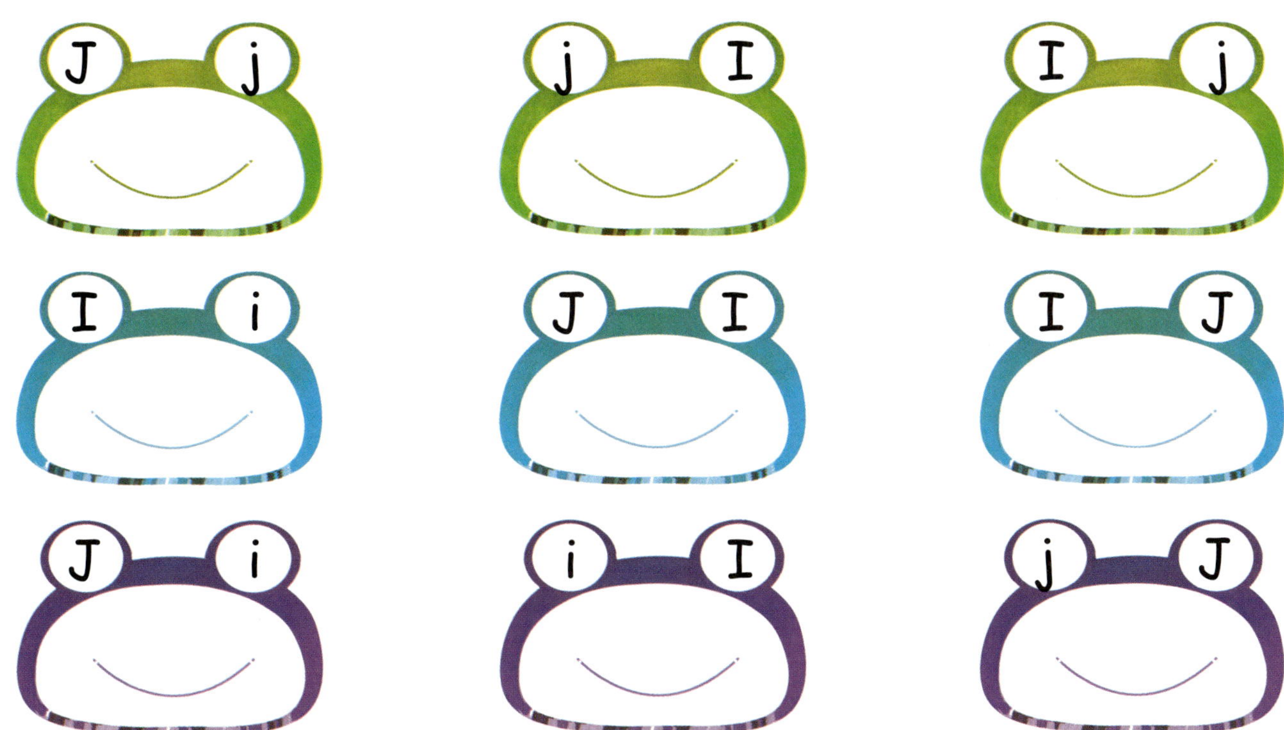

C Circle the right beginning letters for the pictures.

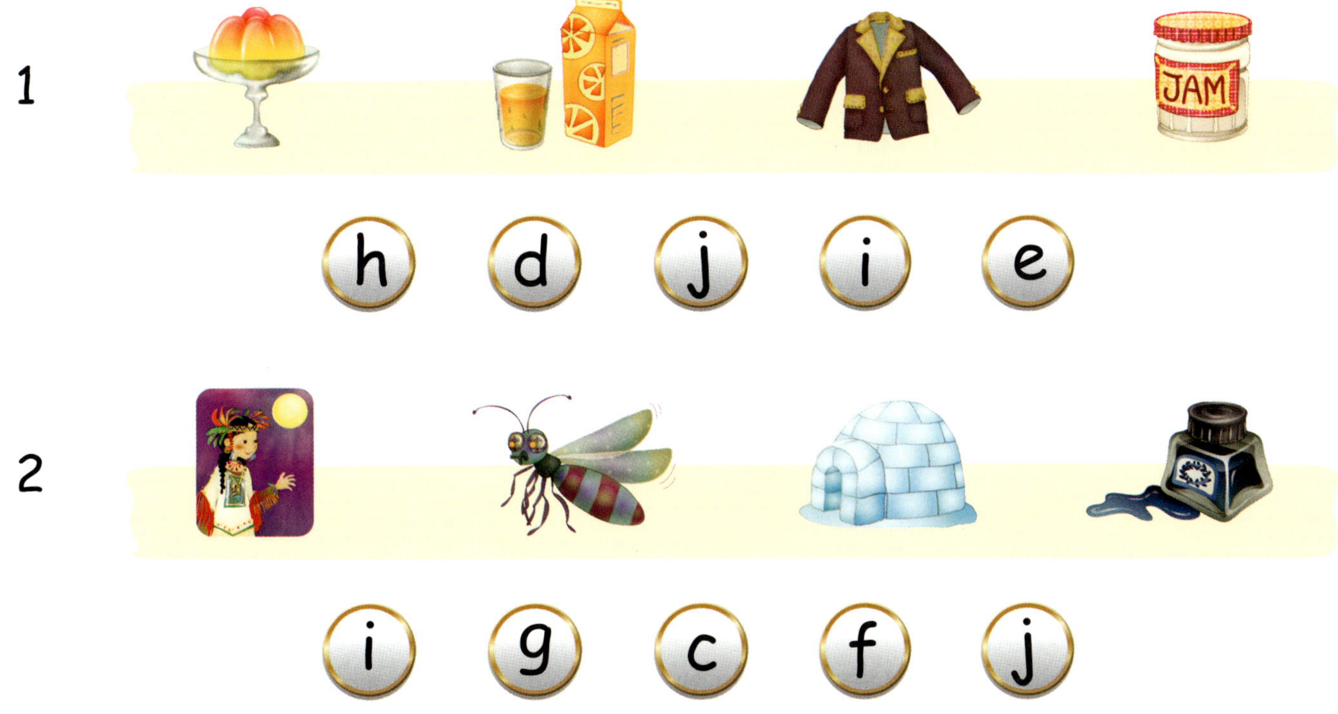

D Check the picture with the right beginning letter.

1

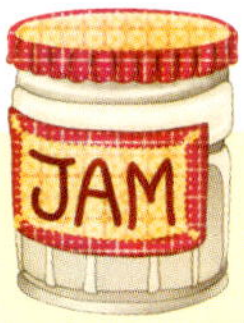

I i

I i

J j

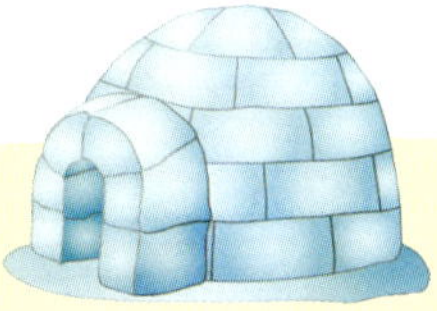

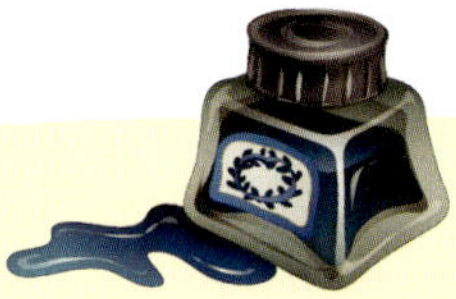

2

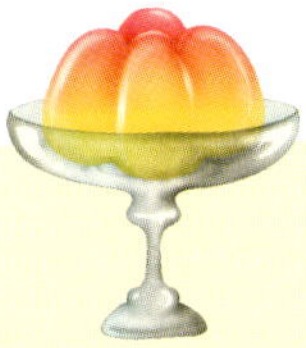

J j

I i

J j

E Match the picture to the beginning letter.

 · · I i · ·

 · · J j · ·

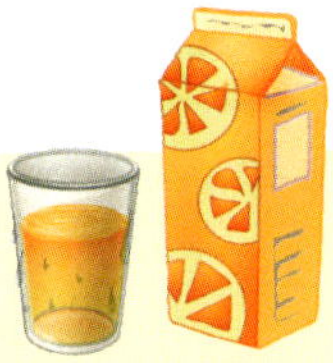

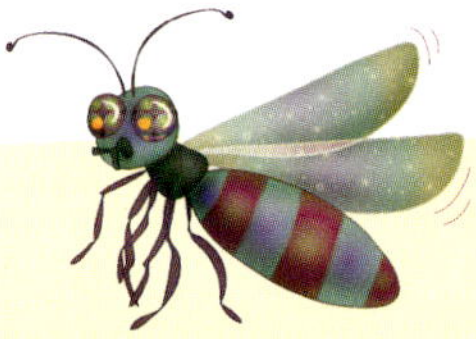

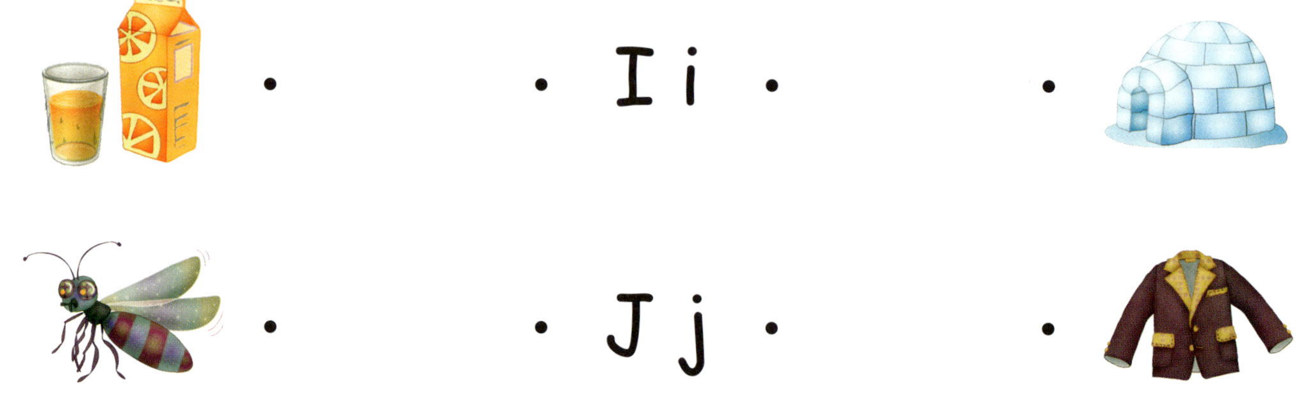

F Write the beginning letter.
Circle the picture with the same beginning letter.

G Say the beginning letters and color the pictures.

K k L l

A Trace and write.

K k

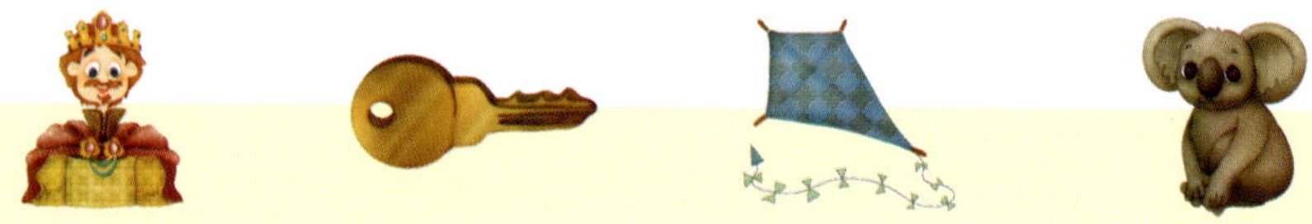

K

k

L l

L

l

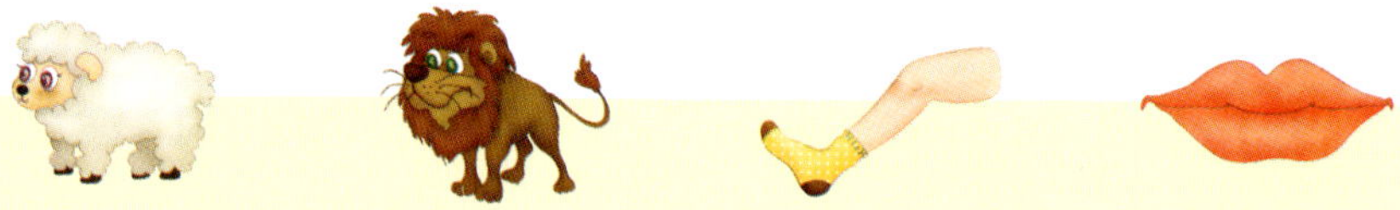

B Color the right pairs.

C Circle the right beginning letters for the pictures.

D Check ✓ the picture with the right beginning letter.

1

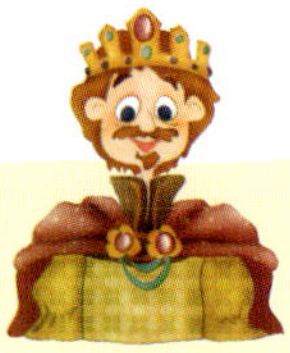

L l	K k	K k
○	○	○

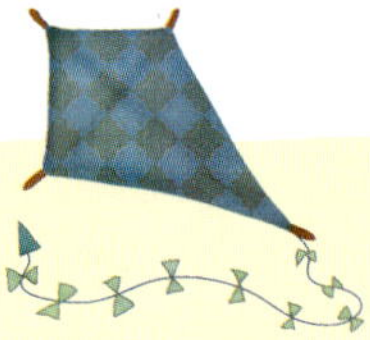

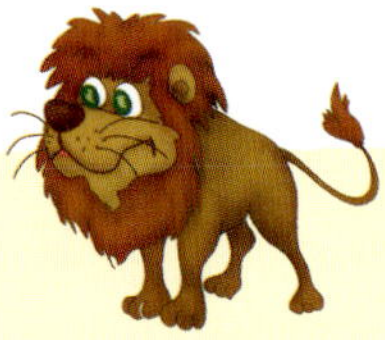

2

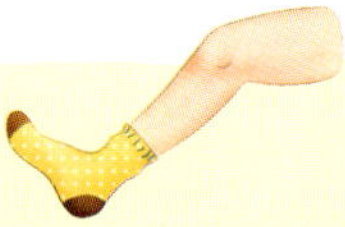

L l	K k	L l
○	○	○

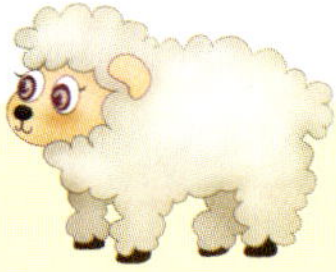

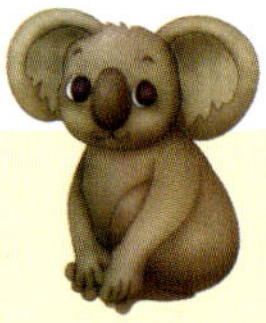

E Match the picture to the beginning letter.

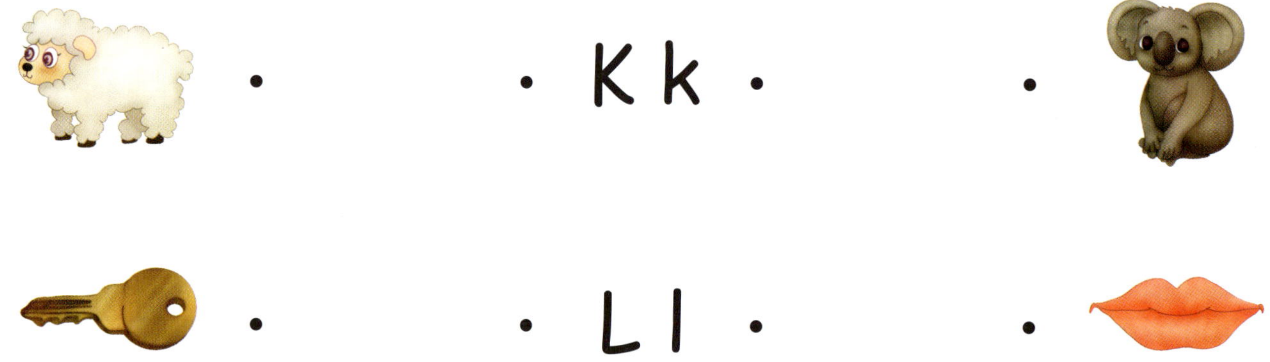

F Write the beginning letter.
Circle the picture with the same beginning letter.

G Say the beginning letters and color the pictures.

Mm Nn

A Trace and write.

Mm

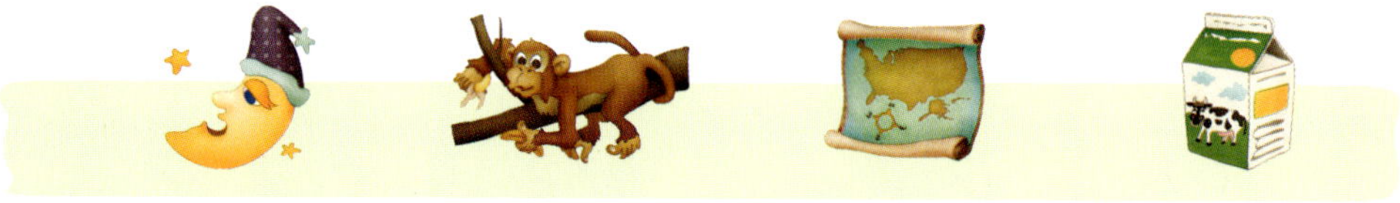

M M M M

m m m m

Nn

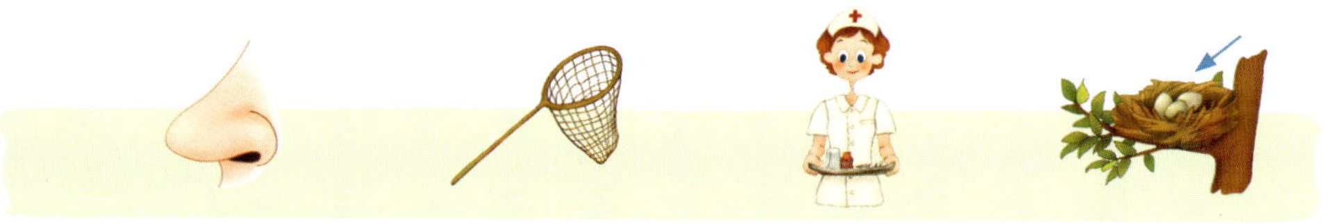

N N N N

n n n n

B Color the right pairs.

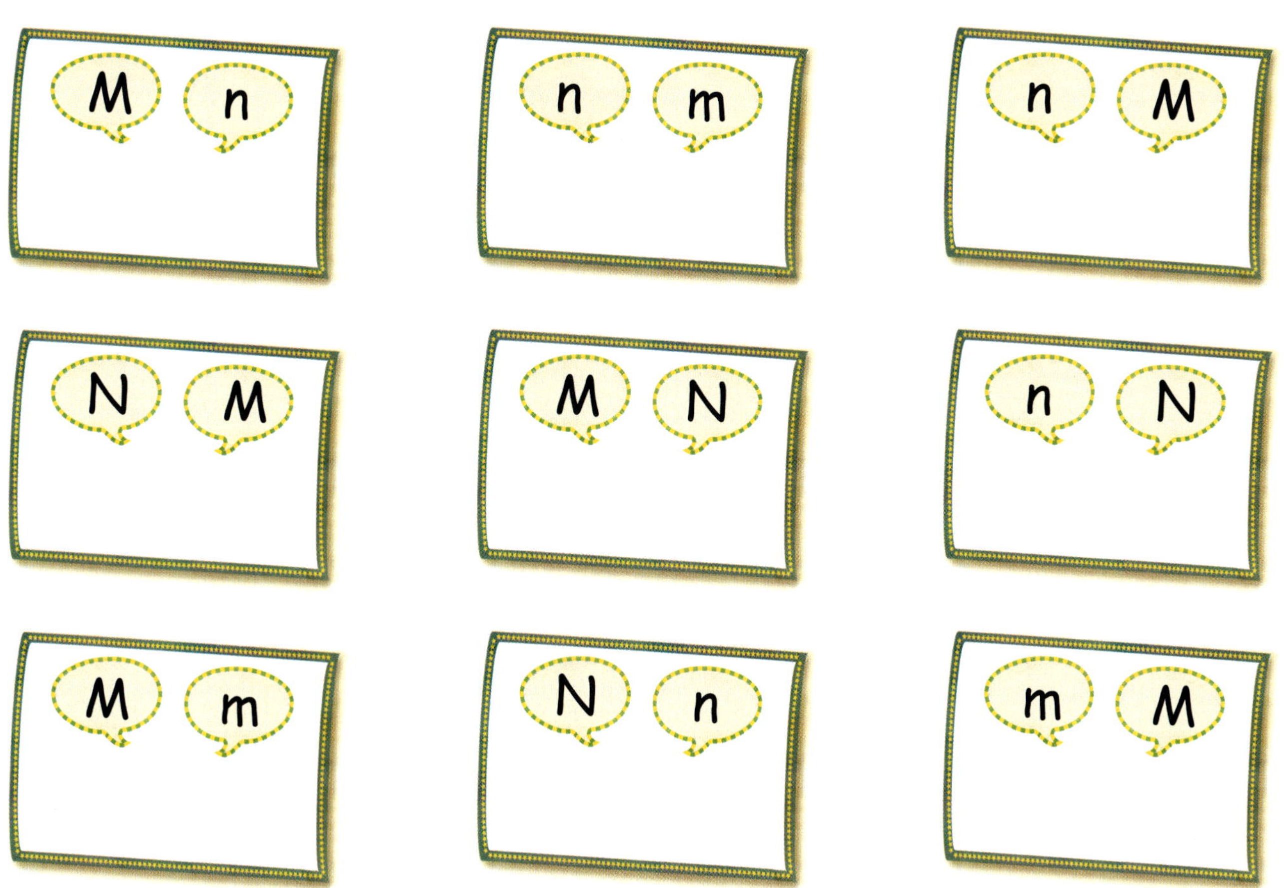

C Circle the right beginning letters for the pictures.

D Check the picture with the right beginning letter.

1

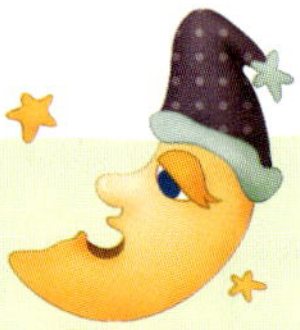

M m

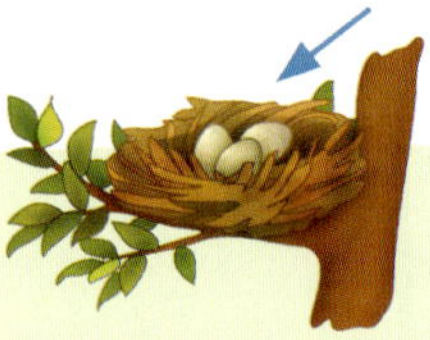

M m

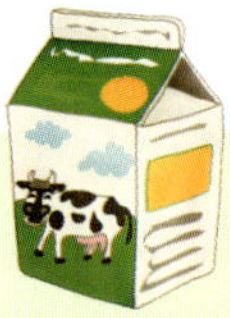

N n

2

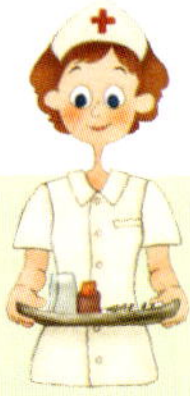

M m

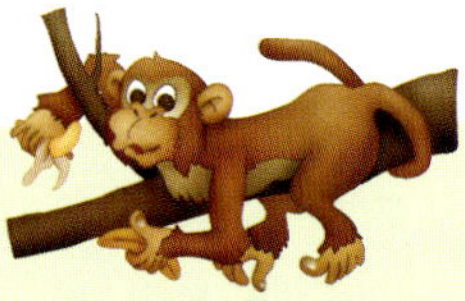

N n

N n

E Match the picture to the beginning letter.

 · · Mm · ·

 · · Nn · ·

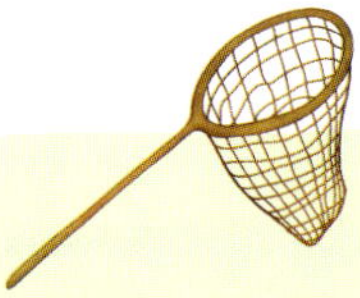

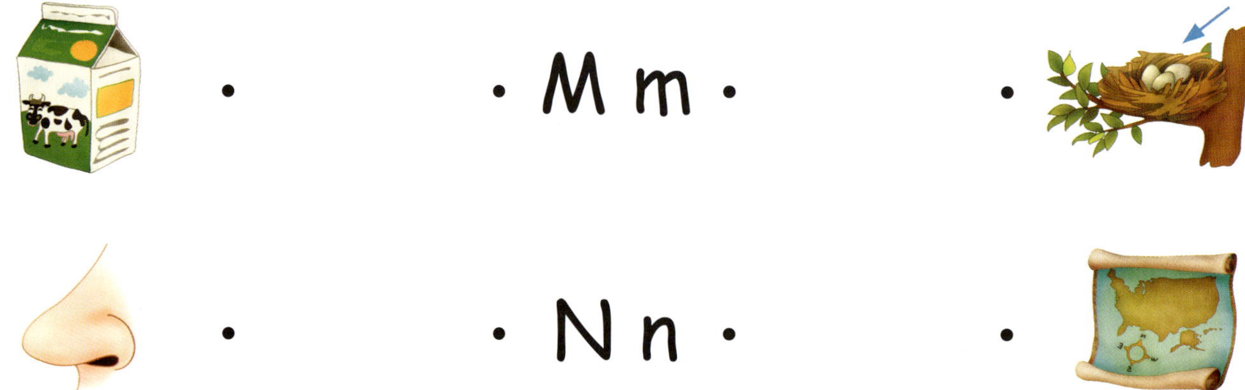

F Write the beginning letter.
Circle the picture with the same beginning letter.

1
2

G Say the beginning letters and color the pictures.

O o P p

A Trace and write.

O o

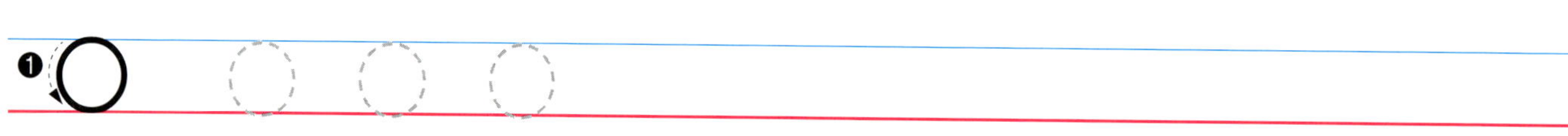

P p

B Color the right pairs.

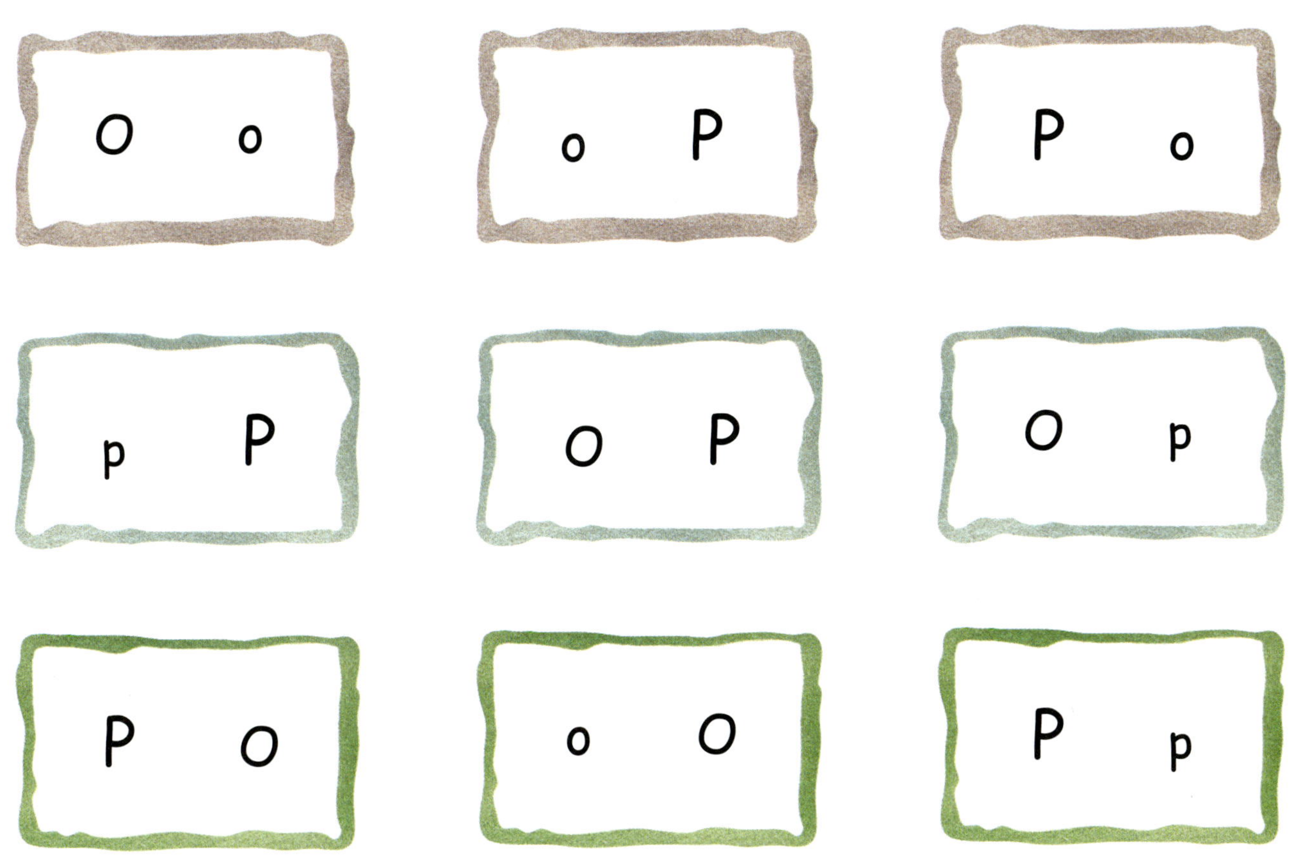

C Circle the right beginning letters for the pictures.

D Check ✓ the picture with the right beginning letter.

1

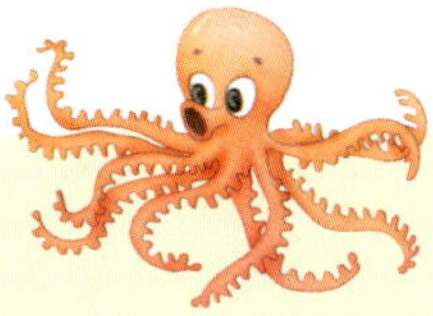

P p	O o	P p
○	○	○

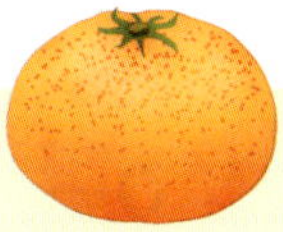

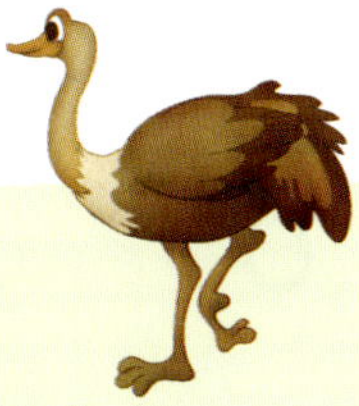

2

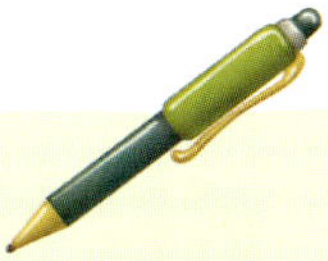

O o	P p	O o
○	○	○

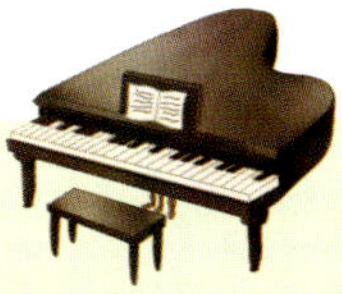

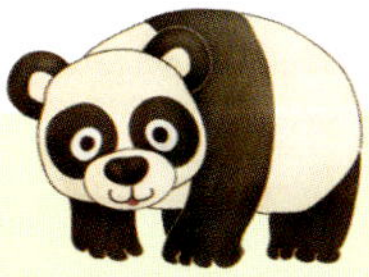

E Match the picture to the beginning letter.

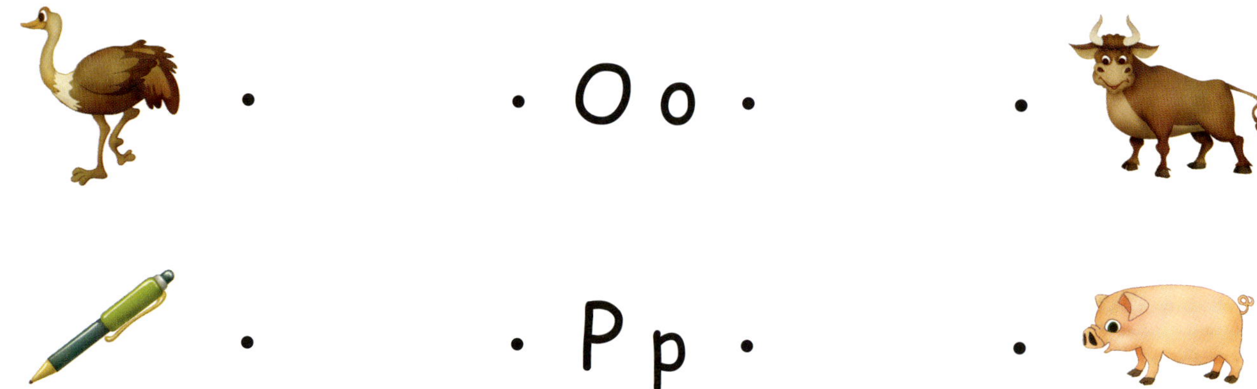

F Write the beginning letter.
Circle the picture with the same beginning letter.

G Say the beginning letters and color the pictures.

UNIT 9

Q q R r

A Trace and write.

Q q

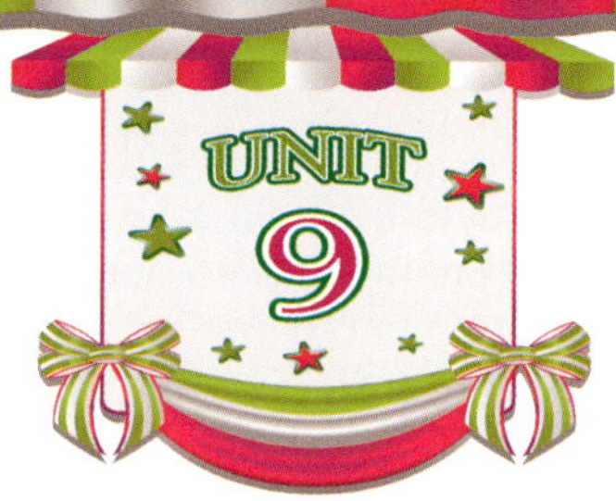

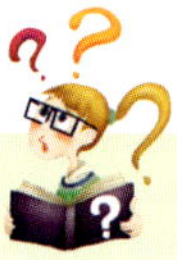 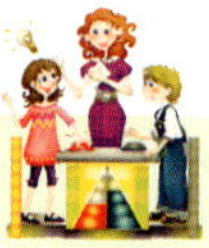 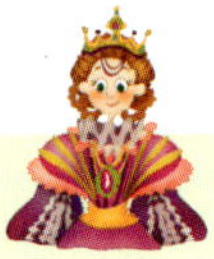 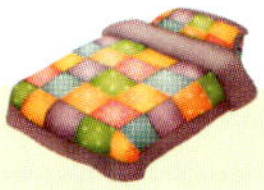

Q Q Q Q

q q q q

R r

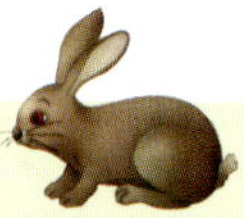 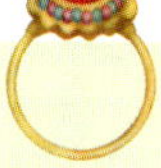 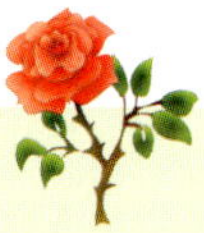 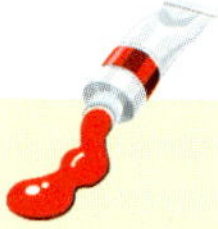

R R R R

r r r r

B Color the right pairs.

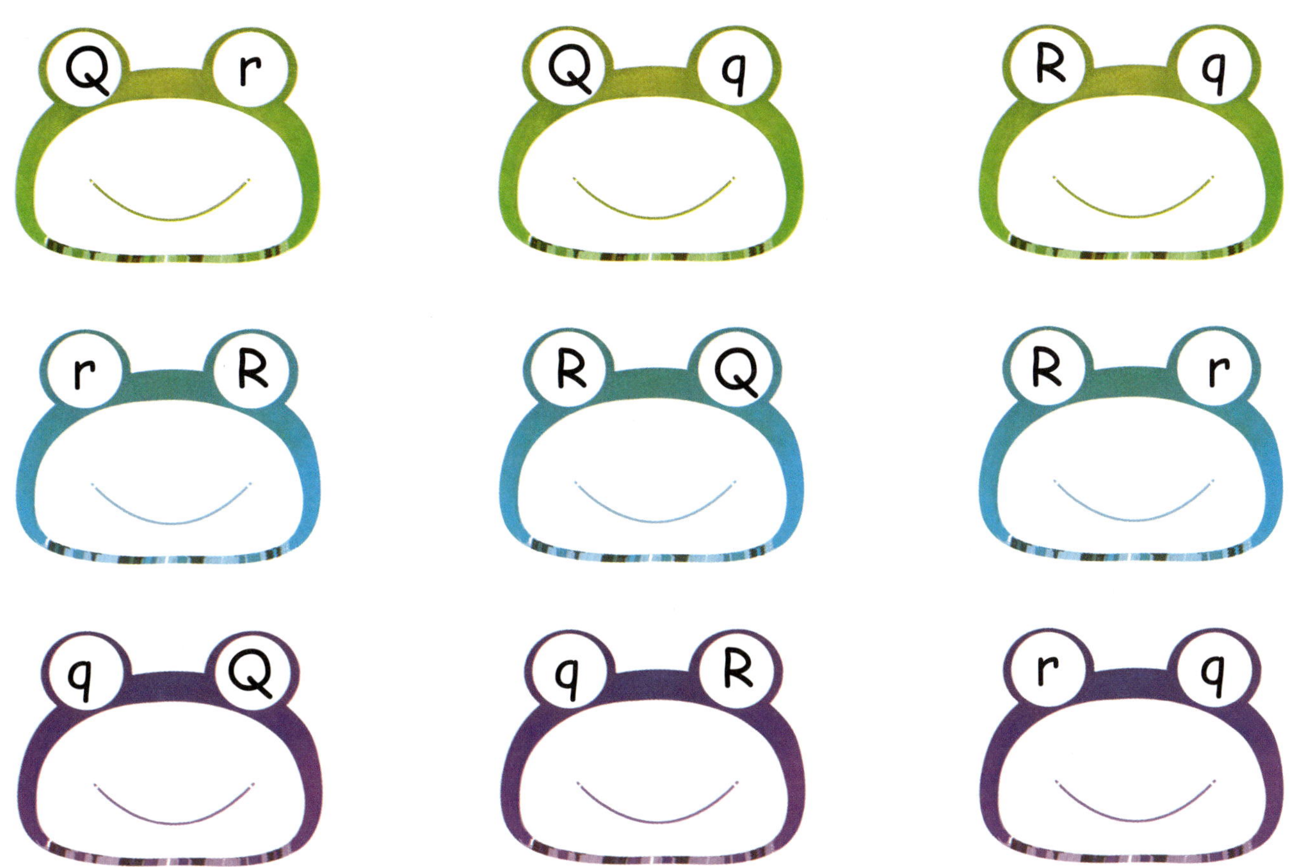

C Circle the right beginning letters for the pictures.

D Check the picture with the right beginning letter.

1

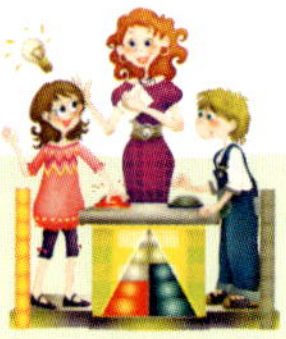

Q q	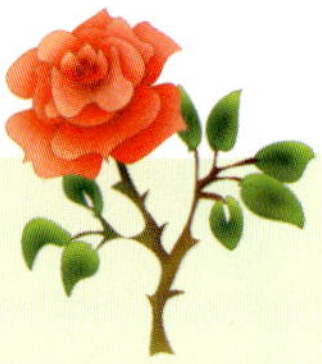 Q q	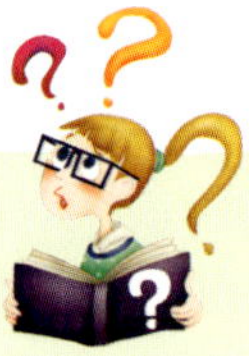 R r
○	○	○

2

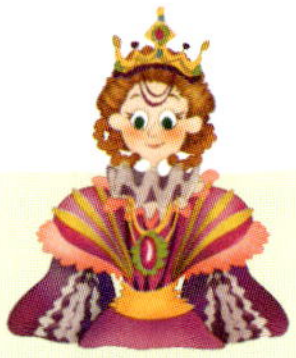

R r	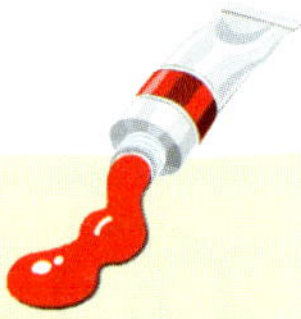 Q q	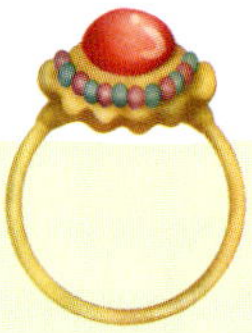 R r
○	○	○

E Match the picture to the beginning letter.

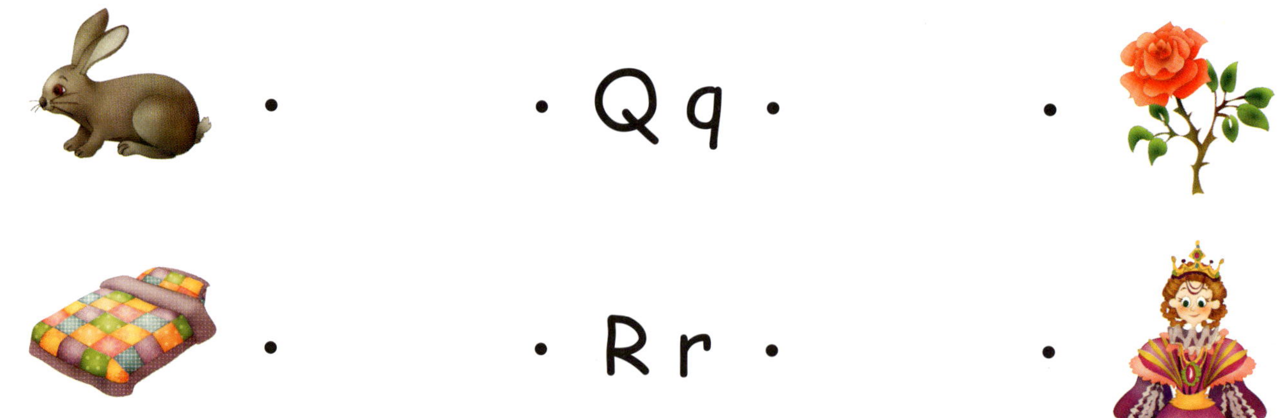

F Write the beginning letter. Circle the picture with the same beginning letter.

G Say the beginning letters and color the pictures.

S s T t

Ⓐ Trace and write.

S s

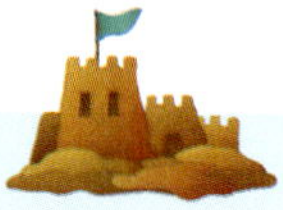

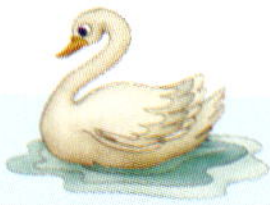

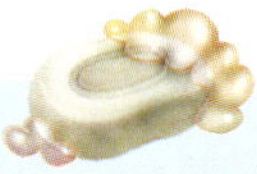

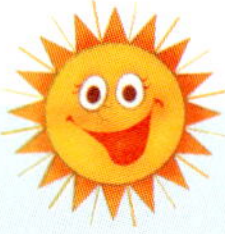

❶ S

❶ s

T t

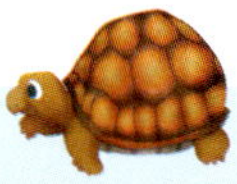

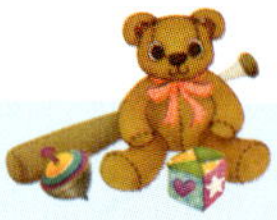

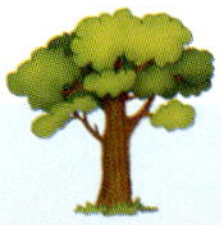

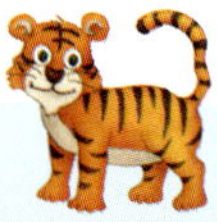

❶ ❷ T

❶ ❷ t

B Color the right pairs.

C Circle the right beginning letters for the pictures.

D Check ✓ the picture with the right beginning letter.

1

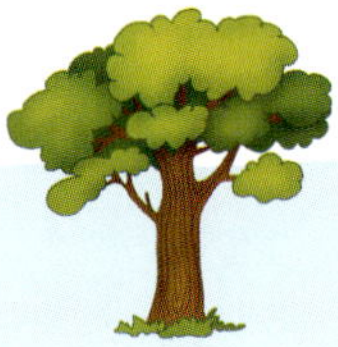

T t

S s

S s

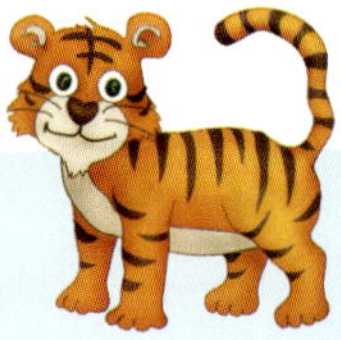

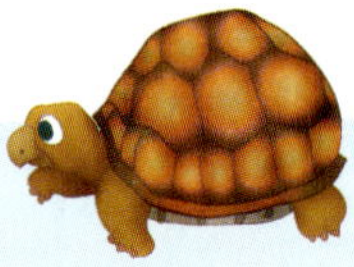

2

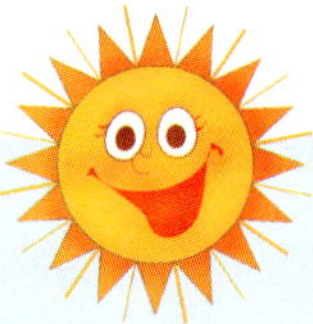

T t

T t

S s

E Match the picture to the beginning letter.

S s

T t

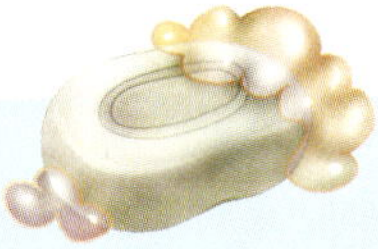

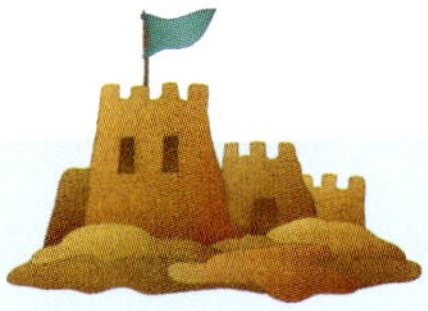

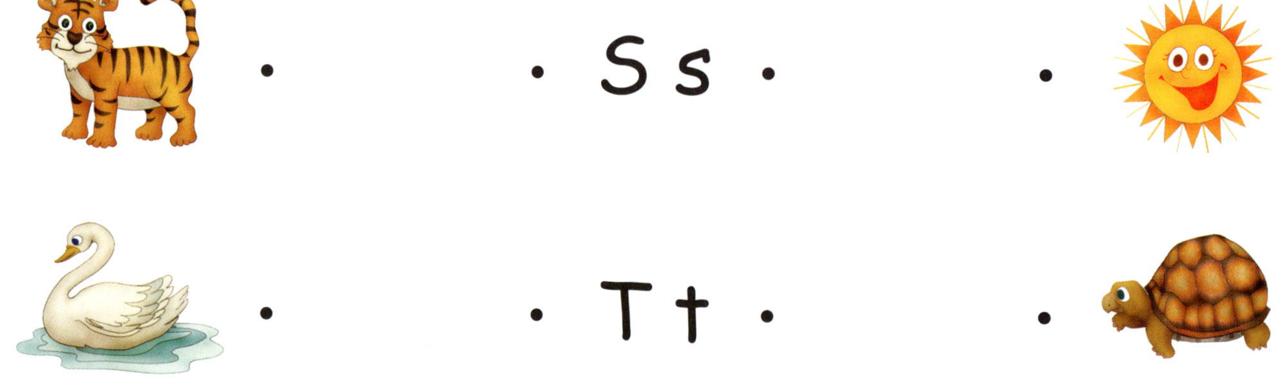

F Write the beginning letter.
Circle the picture with the same beginning letter.

G Say the beginning letters and color the pictures.

UNIT 11

U u V v W w

A Trace and write.

U u

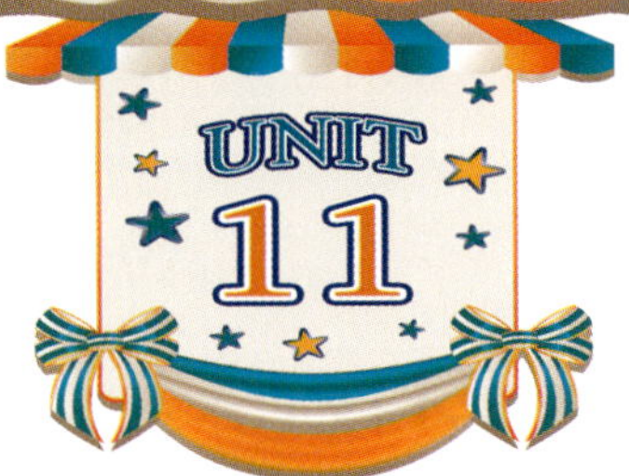

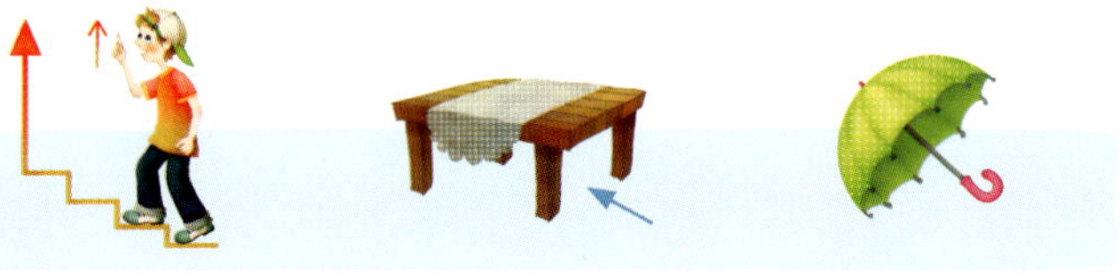

U U U u u u

V v

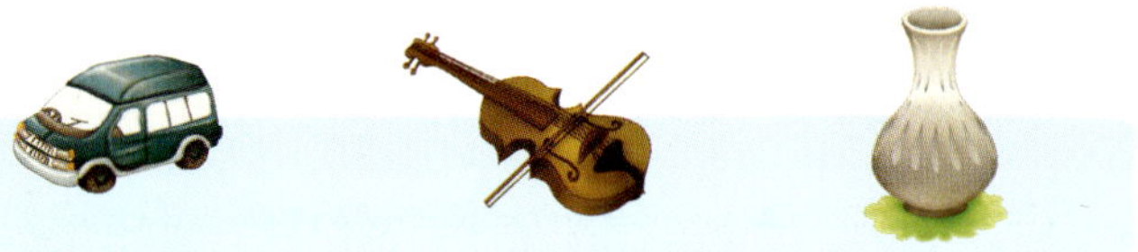

V V V v v v

W w

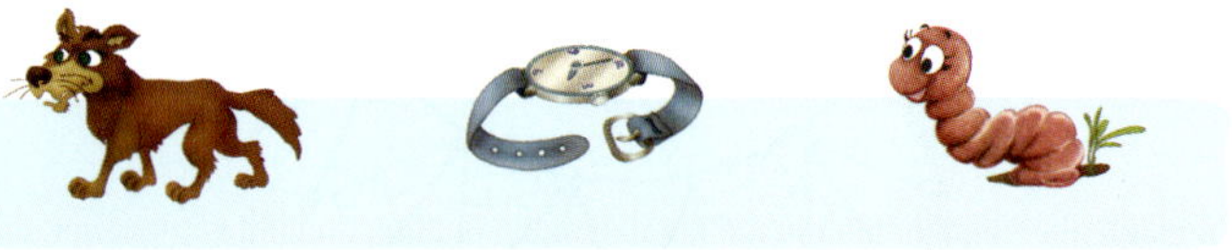

W W W w w w

Ⓑ Color the right pairs.

Ⓒ Circle the right beginning letters for the pictures.

D Check ✔ the picture with the right beginning letter.

1

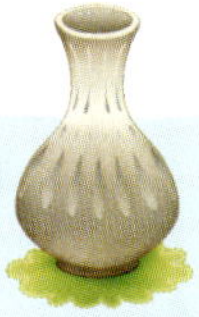

U u ○

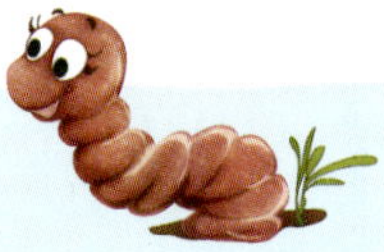

W w ○

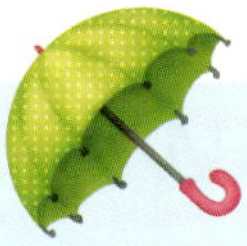

V v ○

2

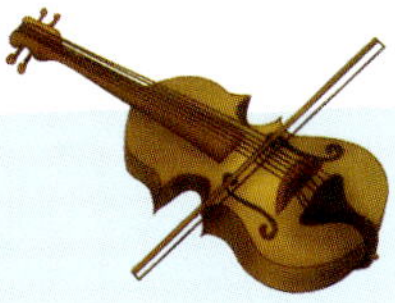

W w ○

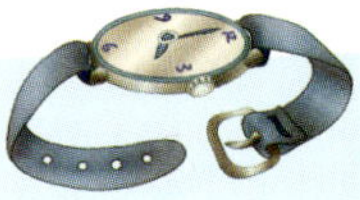

V v ○

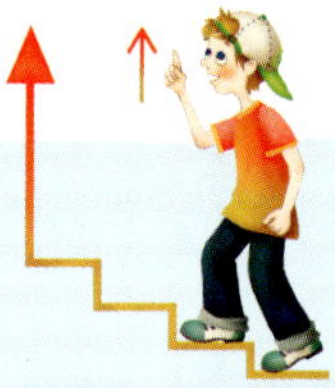

U u ○

3

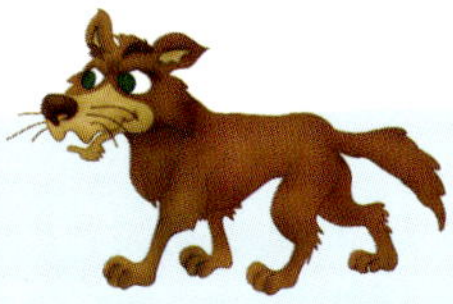

U u ○

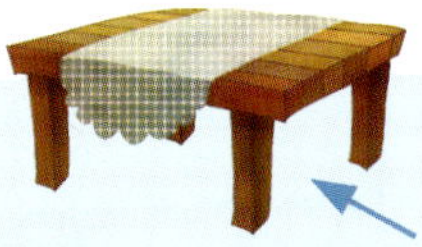

W w ○

V v ○

E Match the picture to the beginning letter.

 • • U u • •

 • • V v • •

 • • W w • •

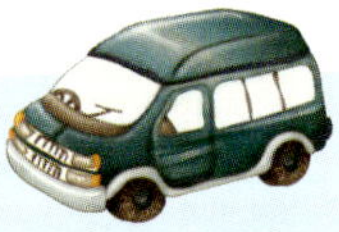

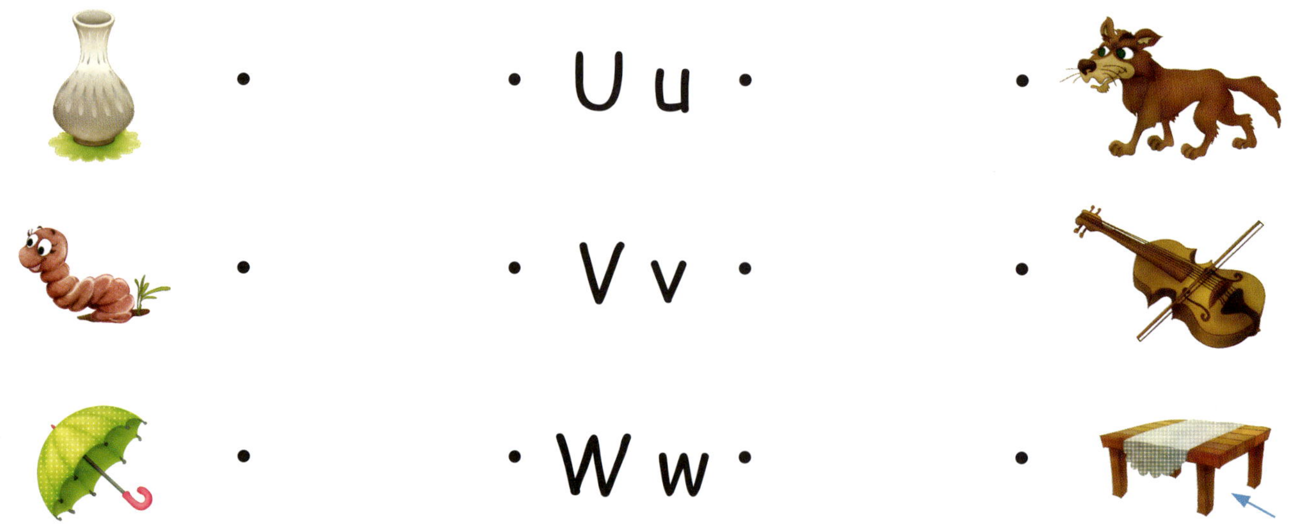

F Write the beginning letter.
Circle the picture with the same beginning letter.

G Say the beginning letters and color the pictures.

UNIT 12

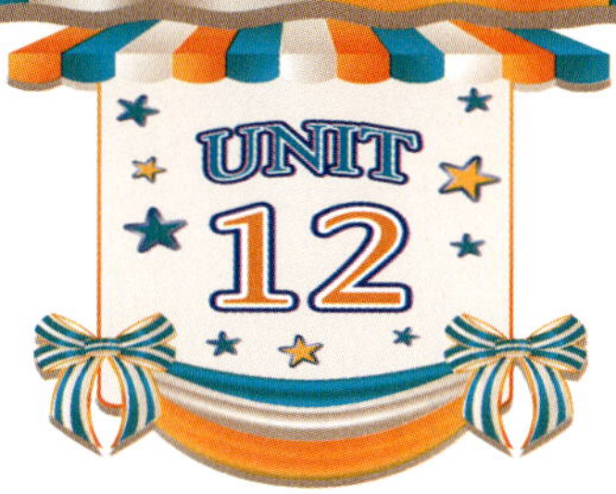

X x Y y Z z

A Trace and write.

X x

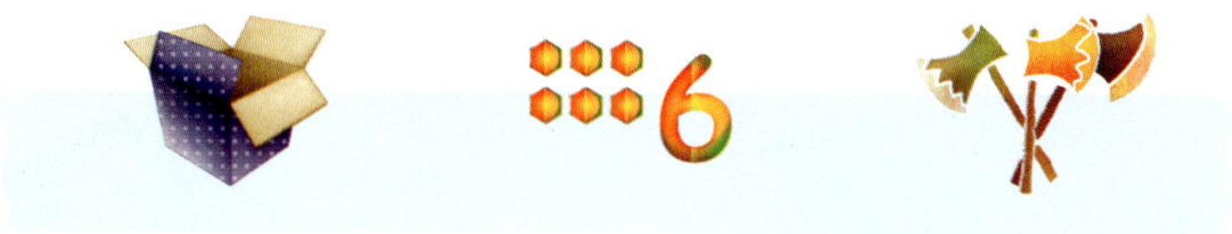

Y y

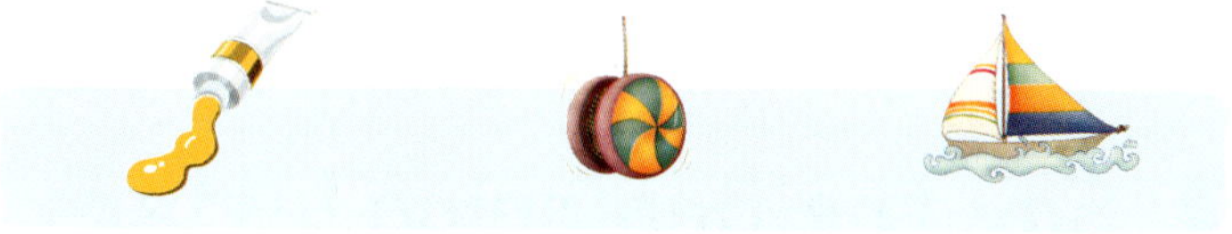

Z z

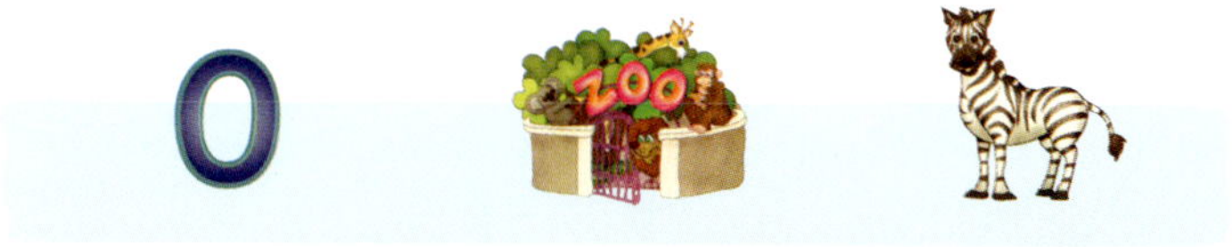

B Color the right pairs.

C Circle the right beginning or ending letters for the pictures.

D Check ✓ the picture with the right beginning or ending letter.

1

Y y ○

Z z ○

X x ○

2

X x ○

Y y ○

Z z ○

3

Y y ○

Z z ○

X x ○

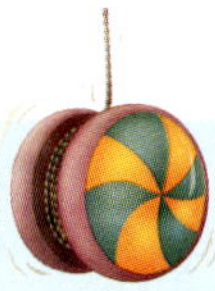

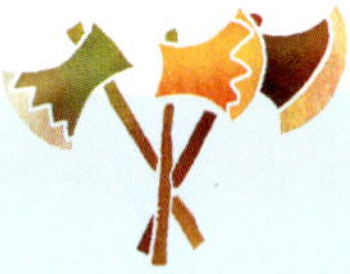

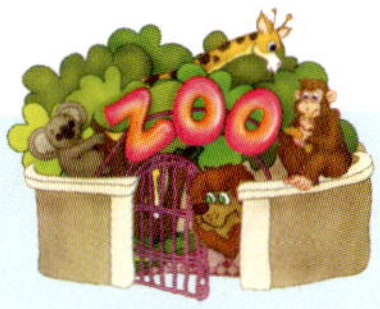

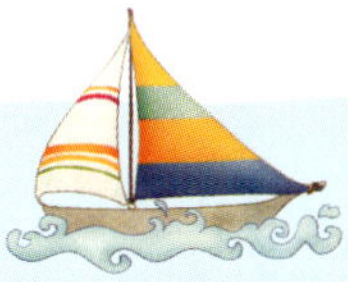

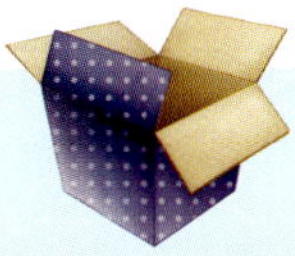

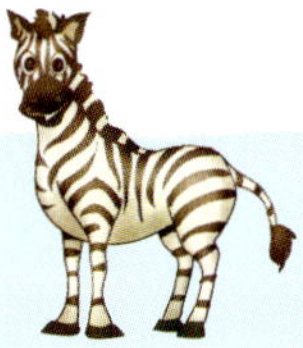

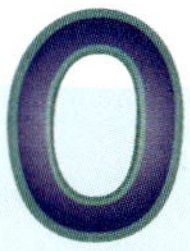

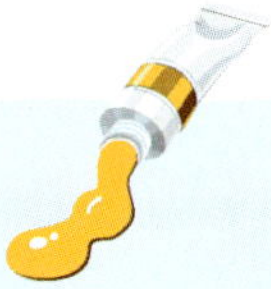

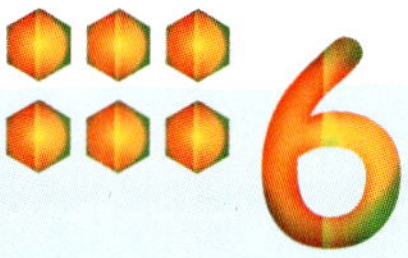

E Match the picture to the beginning or ending letter.

 • • X x • •

 • • Y y • •

 • • Z z • •

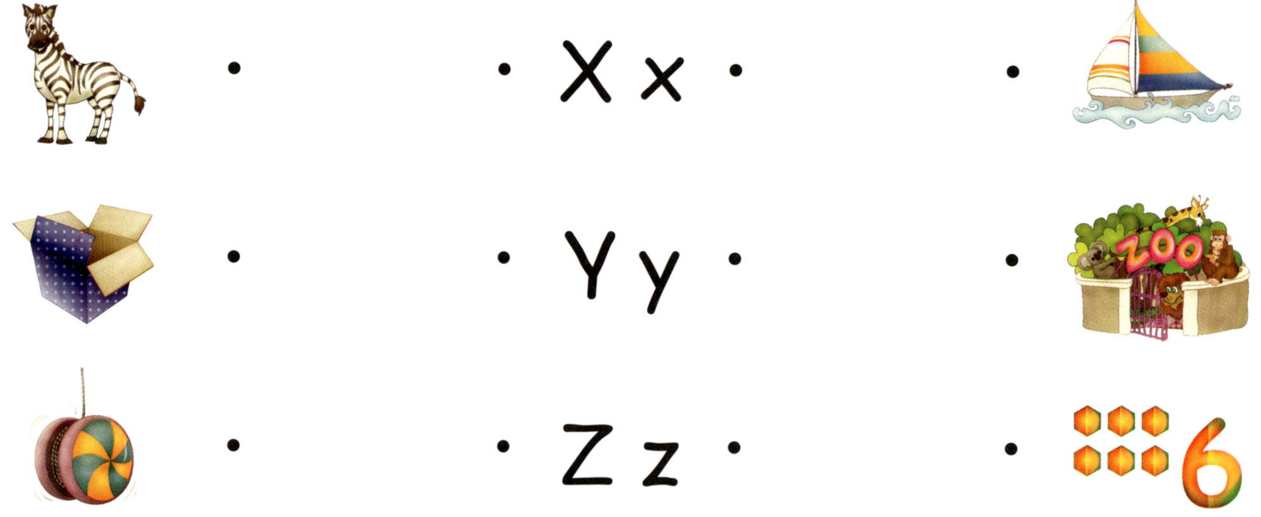

Ⓕ Write the beginning or ending letter. Circle the picture with the same beginning or ending letter.

Ⓖ Say the beginning or ending letters and color the pictures.

CERTIFICATE

Name

Date

Signed

B b	A a
D d	C c
F f	E e
H h	G g

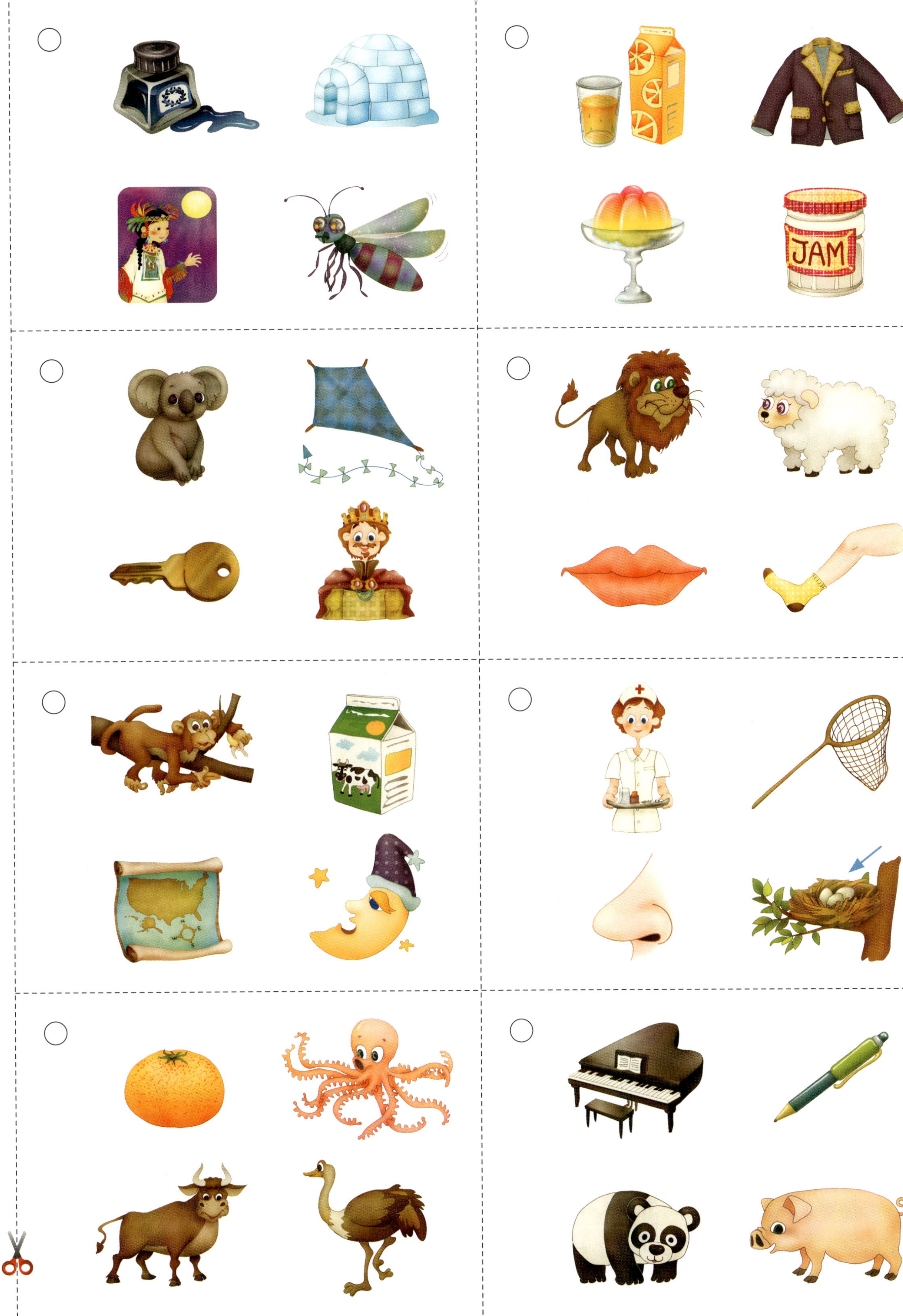
JAM

Jj Ii

Ll Kk

Nn Mm

Pp Oo

R r	Q q
T t	S s
V v	U u
X x	W w

ZOO
O

Z z

Y y

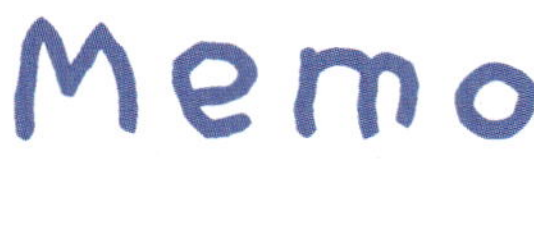

Memo

Phonics PARTY 1

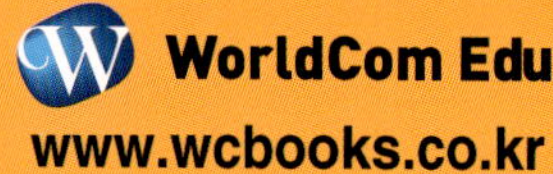
WorldCom Edu
www.wcbooks.co.kr